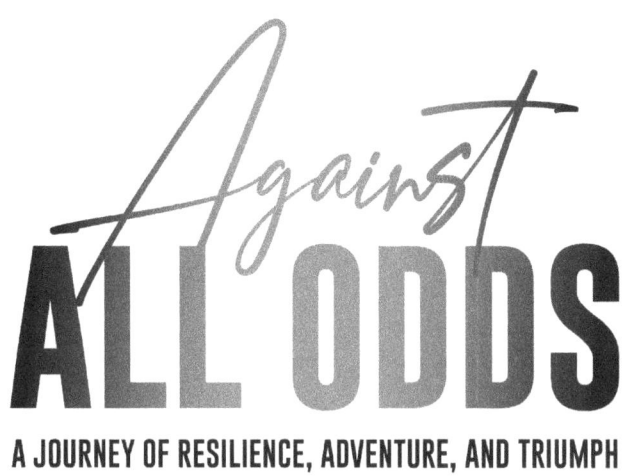

Against ALL ODDS

A JOURNEY OF RESILIENCE, ADVENTURE, AND TRIUMPH

*FROM DUSTBOWL ROOTS TO GLOBAL
ADVENTURES AND LIFE LESSONS*

DALLAS W. THOMPSON

Copyright © 2025 By: Dallas W. Thompson

All rights reserved. No part of this publication may be copied, reproduced in any format, by any means, electronic or otherwise, without prior consent from the copyright owner and publisher of this book.

Published By: Dallas Enterprises USA
6311 Sutter Dr, Lakeside, Arizona 85929
dallas93309@gmail.com
https://www.publishingenterises.com

PREVIOUS BOOKS

1. **Eyes Wide Shut Hide In Plain Sight:** An Enigma
2. **Against All Odds:** A Journey Of Resilience, Adventure, And Triumph From Dust Bowl Roots To Global Adventures And Life Lessons
3. **Yes Mom, I Do Remember:** Memories Of My Past, Provided A Foundation For My Future
4. **Zero Point:** A Sci-Fi Thriller Of Alien Energy And Hidden Wars Energy Is Power. Power Is War
5. **Critical Mass:** The Youtube Generation's Alien War When Digital Natives Meet Extraterrestrial Reality Digital Online
6. **Reality's End:** The Final War For Consciousness Across All Existence A Post-Apocalyptic Space Opera Of Infinite Consciousness And Cosmic War
7. **The Shadow Protocol:** A Mind-Bending Ai Consciousness - Multiverse Science Time Travel And Government Conspiracy
8. **The Prometheus Submarine:** A Quantum Submarine A Deep Sea Military Thriller

Fantasy Romance Series: 9, 10, & 11

9. **Crown Of Shadows:** A Dark Fae Academy Romance Enemies To Lovers Fantasy With Magic And Forbidden Love
10. **Throne Of Starlight:** A Dark Fae Empire Romance An Epic Fantasy Romance
11. **Crown Of Shadows And Starfire:** A Dark Fae Court Romance Dark Fae Romantasy

12. **Crypto:** The Digital Guardian An Ai Techno-Thriller

Books In A Series: 13, 14, 15, 16, & 17

13. **The Universal Mind:** Consciousness As The Fundamental Fabric Of Reality A Revolutionary Paradigm For Understanding Consciousness, Reality, And Human Destiny
14. **Reality: What Is It?** The Nature Of Reality: Philosophical And Scientific Investigations
15. **The Observer-Reality Nexus:** How Consciousness And The Physical World Co-Create Each Other
16. **The Quantum Frontier:** Exploring The Known, Unknown, And Unknowable In Modern Physics
17. **Retrocausality In Quantum Physics:** A New Framework For Time, Causality, And Reality

Children's Books #18, & 19

18. **Lilypad And The Quest For The Glimmering Gears:** A Stem Adventure About Courage, Friendship, And Following Your Dreams
19. **Pip The Wiggle - Waggle:** Ages 4 To 7, 100 Word Vocabulary

WHAT OTHERS ARE SAYING ABOUT AGAINST ALL ODDS: A JOURNEY OF RESILIENCE, ADVENTURE, AND TRIUMPH

"Thompson's memoir reads like an American epic wrapped in the dust and dreams of the Great Depression. From his Dust Bowl origins in Weedpatch to sailing bamboo rafts across the Pacific, this is storytelling at its most authentic and inspiring. His unflinching honesty about failure, success, and the true meaning of wealth makes this essential reading for anyone seeking to understand the American entrepreneurial spirit. Thompson proves that resilience isn't just about surviving—it's about thriving against all odds." - Jennifer Hudson, Business Owner, PhD

"Against All Odds is a masterclass in American resilience literature. Thompson's journey from poverty to prosperity and back again illuminates the complex relationship between identity, success, and self-worth in modern America. His experiences span from the historical Dust Bowl migration to contemporary entrepreneurship, creating a unique bridge between past and present. This memoir deserves a place alongside the great American autobiographies—it's both deeply personal and universally relevant." - Dr. Sarah Mithel, Professor of American Studies

"A remarkable testament to the power of reinvention. Thompson's narrative voice is both humble and confident, never shying away from his failures while celebrating his triumphs with genuine gratitude. His adventures—from building bamboo rafts in Fiji to teaching Apache children—read like fiction but carry the weight of lived truth. This is memoir writing at its finest: honest, engaging, and ultimately transformative for both author and reader." - Wayne Stephens, Real Estate Developer, MBA

"Dallas Thompson embodies everything I teach about financial education and entrepreneurial thinking. His story proves that true wealth isn't measured in dollars but in experiences, relationships, and the courage to keep reinventing yourself. From Honda dealerships to real estate empires to teaching children, Thompson shows us that success has many faces. This book should be required reading for anyone serious about understanding money, business, and life." - Doyle Robertson, Author, MBA, Professor

"Thompson's memoir transcends the typical rags-to-riches narrative by exploring the psychological and spiritual dimensions of success and failure. His candid discussions of overachievement, identity crisis, and finding purpose beyond wealth creation offer profound insights into the American Dream's complexities. The book's structure—moving from childhood poverty through multiple careers and retirements—creates a compelling arc that will resonate with readers across generations. Highly recommended for biography collections and entrepreneurship sections."
- Wallace Jackson, MBA

FOREWORD

By Dr. Leroy Chang, Professor of Entrepreneurship
In the pantheon of American autobiographies, certain narratives transcend mere personal recollection to become cultural touchstones that illuminate the broader human experience. Dallas W. Thompson's "Against All Odds: A Journey of Resilience, Adventure, and Triumph" stands as such a work—a memoir that captures not only one man's extraordinary journey but also the essence of American resilience, entrepreneurship, and the relentless pursuit of reinvention that defines our national character.

As someone who has spent decades studying entrepreneurial psychology and the socioeconomic dynamics of American success stories, I find Thompson's narrative particularly compelling because it defies the conventional wisdom about wealth, achievement, and personal fulfillment. His story begins in the dust-choked fields of Depression-era California, among the "Okies" whose struggles John Steinbeck immortalized in "The Grapes of Wrath." Yet Thompson's memoir is not merely another rags-to-riches tale; it is a profound meditation on the cyclical nature of success and failure, and the courage required to embrace both with equal grace.

What sets Thompson's story apart is his unflinching honesty about the psychological toll of extreme success and the disorientation that comes with achieving one's wildest dreams. His candid exploration of what he terms "overachievement"—the phenomenon of surpassing one's own ambitions to the point of existential confusion—offers invaluable insights into the modern American condition. In an era where entrepreneurial success is often mythologized and simplified, Thompson's nuanced examination of wealth's psychological impact provides a necessary counterbalance to prevailing narratives.

The memoir's structure mirrors the complexity of Thompson's journey itself. From his early years in Weedpatch, where poverty was "a constant companion," through his service as a top-secret Air Force cryptographer, to his meteoric rise as a Honda dealer and real estate mogul, Thompson's narrative demonstrates the multifaceted nature of American opportunity. His ability to reinvent himself repeatedly—from businessman to educator, from entrepreneur to adventurer—speaks to a fundamental American trait: the belief that we are not bound by our circumstances but empowered to transcend them.

Perhaps most remarkably, Thompson's adventures extend far beyond the boardroom. His decision to build a fifty-foot bamboo raft in Fiji and attempt to sail it to Australia reads like something from a Jack London novel, yet it represents a deeper truth about the entrepreneurial spirit: the need to test oneself against impossible odds, to push beyond the boundaries of conventional experience. These adventures are not mere diversions from his business career but integral expressions of the same restless energy that drove his professional success.

Thompson's later transition to education, particularly his work teaching Apache children at Fort Apache, reveals another dimension of his character that enriches the entire narrative. His discovery of his own

Native American heritage and his grandmother's shame about her identity adds layers of complexity to his understanding of American identity and belonging. This section of the memoir demonstrates how personal growth often requires us to confront uncomfortable truths about our past and our society's treatment of marginalized communities.

The memoir's treatment of failure is perhaps its greatest strength. Thompson's loss of millions during the 1980s recession and his subsequent battles with the IRS could have been portrayed as mere setbacks on the road to eventual triumph. Instead, Thompson uses these experiences to explore fundamental questions about identity, self-worth, and the relationship between external success and internal fulfillment. His observation that "failure is a description of an event" rather than a judgment on personal worth offers a profound reframing that will resonate with readers facing their own challenges.

Thompson's writing style reflects his background and personality—direct, unpretentious, and grounded in practical experience. He avoids the self-aggrandizement that mars many entrepreneurial memoirs, instead offering a clear-eyed assessment of his strengths, weaknesses, and the role of luck in his various successes. His voice carries the authenticity of someone who has lived through genuine hardship and emerged with hard-won wisdom rather than easy platitudes.

The memoir's exploration of relationships—particularly Thompson's reunion with his childhood sweetheart after forty-two years and their marriage in their later years—adds emotional depth to what could have been merely a business narrative. Their shared battle with her cancer and their current adventures in retirement demonstrate that life's most meaningful chapters often come after traditional measures of success have been achieved or abandoned.

From an academic perspective, Thompson's memoir provides valuable insights into several important areas of study. His experiences during the Dust Bowl migration offer firsthand testimony to one of America's most significant internal migrations. His work in military intelligence during the Cold War, while necessarily limited by security considerations, provides glimpses into the psychological pressures faced by those who served in classified roles. His entrepreneurial journey illustrates the practical application of business principles across multiple industries and economic cycles.

The memoir also serves as a case study in resilience and adaptability. Thompson's ability to rebuild after catastrophic losses, to find meaning in teaching after achieving financial independence, and to embrace new adventures in his eighties demonstrates the kind of psychological flexibility that researchers have identified as crucial for long-term success and happiness. His story provides a roadmap for others facing major life transitions or seeking to redefine success on their own terms.

For contemporary readers, Thompson's memoir offers particularly relevant insights into the relationship between work and identity. His struggle with the question "Who am I without work?" when he achieved financial independence at thirty-three speaks directly to current discussions about purpose, meaning, and the future of work in an automated economy. His eventual answer—that identity must be grounded in self-acceptance rather than external achievement—provides a framework for navigating these challenges.

The memoir's treatment of wealth and materialism is refreshingly nuanced. Thompson neither demonizes money nor worships it, instead presenting it as a tool that can provide freedom and opportunities while also creating new forms of pressure and responsibility. His observation that "having money gives one more choice" while emphasizing that "it is not a measure of success" reflects a mature understanding of wealth's role in human flourishing.

Thompson's adventures in the South Pacific, particularly his time in Fiji building the bamboo raft, offer more than exotic entertainment. They represent a deliberate choice to step outside the comfort zone of American middle-class life and engage with different cultures and ways of being. His respectful but honest portrayal of Fijian village life, including its challenges and contradictions, demonstrates the kind of cultural curiosity and openness that enriches both travel and life.

The memoir's final chapters, focusing on Thompson's current life with his wife Connie, their Airbnb business, and their plans for continued exploration, provide a hopeful vision of aging that counters prevailing narratives of decline and limitation. Their approach to retirement as a new adventure rather than a withdrawal from life offers inspiration for readers of all ages.

In recommending this memoir to readers, I would emphasize its value not just as entertainment but as a source of practical wisdom about resilience, reinvention, and the pursuit of meaningful life. Thompson's story demonstrates that success is not a destination but a process, not a single achievement but a series of adaptations to changing circumstances. His journey from poverty to wealth to purpose illustrates the American Dream's complexity while affirming its continued relevance.

"Against All Odds" deserves a place among the great American memoirs not because Thompson achieved extraordinary wealth or fame, but because he lived an extraordinarily examined life and had the courage to share its lessons with honesty and humility. In an era of increasing polarization and uncertainty, his story reminds us of the values that have long sustained American society: hard work, resilience, adaptability, and the belief that we can always begin again.

Dr. Leroy Chang, Professor of Entrepreneurship

INTRODUCTION

"Against All Odds: A Journey of Resilience, Adventure, and Triumph" emerges from the American heartland as both a deeply personal memoir and a broader meditation on the nature of success, failure, and reinvention in contemporary life. Dallas W. Thompson's extraordinary journey from Dust Bowl poverty to entrepreneurial success, from devastating loss to meaningful purpose, offers readers a unique window into the complexities of the American Dream and the resilience of the human spirit.

This memoir distinguishes itself from conventional success narratives through its unflinching examination of what Thompson calls the "phenomenon of overachievement"—the disorienting experience of surpassing one's own ambitions and the existential questions that arise when external goals are met but internal fulfillment remains elusive. Thompson's candid exploration of these psychological dimensions adds depth and nuance to what might otherwise be a straightforward rags-to-riches tale.

The narrative spans eight decades of American life, from the Great Depression through the digital age, providing readers with both historical context and timeless wisdom. Thompson's experiences as a child of Dust Bowl refugees, immortalized in John Steinbeck's "The Grapes of Wrath," ground his story in one of America's most significant internal migrations. His subsequent journey through military service during the Cold War, entrepreneurial ventures across multiple industries, and eventual transition to education creates a comprehensive portrait of American opportunity and challenge.

What sets this memoir apart is Thompson's willingness to examine failure with the same honesty and detail he brings to his successes. His loss of millions during the 1980s recession, his battles with the Internal Revenue Service, and his struggles with identity and purpose during periods of transition are presented not as mere obstacles overcome, but as integral parts of a life fully lived. This approach offers readers a more complete and realistic understanding of what it means to pursue ambitious goals in an uncertain world.

The memoir's structure reflects Thompson's belief in the importance of process over outcome. Rather than organizing his story around achievements or chronological milestones, he presents his life as a series of learning experiences, each building upon the last to create a comprehensive education in resilience, adaptability, and personal growth. This approach allows readers to extract practical wisdom from his experiences while appreciating the unique circumstances that shaped his particular journey.

Thompson's adventures beyond the business world—particularly his construction of a fifty-foot bamboo raft in Fiji and his attempt to sail it to Australia—serve as more than colorful interludes in an entrepreneurial narrative. These experiences represent a fundamental aspect of his character: the need to test himself against impossible odds and to seek meaning through direct engagement with the world's challenges and mysteries. They also demonstrate the kind of curiosity and courage that enabled his business successes.

The memoir's treatment of relationships adds emotional depth to what could have been merely a professional narrative. Thompson's reunion with his childhood sweetheart after forty-two years, their marriage in their later years, and their shared battle with her cancer illustrate the ways in which personal connections can provide meaning and purpose that transcend material achievement. Their current life together, managing an Airbnb business and planning new adventures in their eighties, offers a hopeful vision of aging as continued growth rather than gradual decline.

From a historical perspective, Thompson's memoir provides valuable firsthand testimony to several significant periods in American history. His childhood in Weedpatch during the aftermath of the Dust Bowl offers insights into the experiences of internal migrants who shaped California's agricultural development. His service in military intelligence during the Cold War, while necessarily limited by security considerations, provides glimpses into the psychological pressures faced by those who served in classified roles during a period of global tension.

His entrepreneurial journey illustrates the practical application of business principles across multiple industries and economic cycles. From his early success as a Honda dealer to his ventures in real estate development and construction, Thompson's experiences demonstrate both the opportunities available to determined individuals and the risks inherent in ambitious undertakings. His ability to rebuild after catastrophic losses provides a case study in resilience and adaptability that will resonate with readers facing their own challenges.

The memoir's exploration of education and mentorship, particularly Thompson's work teaching Apache children at Fort Apache, reveals another dimension of his character and offers insights into the challenges facing Native American communities. His discovery of his own Native American heritage and his grandmother's shame about her identity adds layers of complexity to his understanding of American identity and belonging.

Thompson's writing style reflects his background and personality—direct, unpretentious, and grounded in practical experience. He avoids the self-aggrandizement that mars many entrepreneurial memoirs, instead offering a clear-eyed assessment of his strengths, weaknesses, and the role of luck in his various successes. His voice carries the authenticity of someone who has lived through genuine hardship and emerged with hard-won wisdom rather than easy platitudes.

The memoir's relevance to contemporary readers extends beyond its historical value or entertainment appeal. Thompson's struggles with questions of identity, purpose, and meaning speak directly to current discussions about the balance of work-life balance, the future of careers in an automated economy, and the relationship between material success and personal fulfillment. His eventual answer—that identity must be grounded in self-acceptance rather than external achievement—provides a framework for navigating these challenges. For entrepreneurs and business leaders, Thompson's memoir offers practical insights into risk management, opportunity recognition, and the psychological dimensions of success and failure. His experiences across multiple industries and economic cycles provide a comprehensive education in the realities of business ownership and the importance of adaptability in changing markets.

For readers interested in adventure and exploration, Thompson's travels and experiences in the South Pacific offer more than exotic entertainment. They represent a deliberate choice to step outside the comfort zone of American middle-class life and engage with different cultures and ways of being. His respectful but honest portrayal of life in Fiji and the Cook Islands demonstrates the kind of cultural curiosity and openness that enriches both travel and life.

The memoir's treatment of aging and retirement challenges conventional narratives about life's later chapters. Thompson and his wife's approach to their eighties as a time for new adventures rather than gradual withdrawal from life offers inspiration for readers of all ages. Their continued engagement with business through their Airbnb, their plans for travel and exploration, and their openness to new experiences demonstrate that life's possibilities do not diminish with age but simply take new forms.

Throughout the narrative, Thompson returns to fundamental questions about the nature of success and the sources of meaning in human life. His observation that "success is unconditional love of oneself" reflects a mature understanding that transcends material achievement while acknowledging its importance. His journey from poverty to wealth to purpose illustrates the evolution of values and priorities that often accompanies a life fully lived.

The memoir also serves as a meditation on the American Dream, not in its simplified form as a guarantee of success for those who work hard, but in its more complex reality as a promise of opportunity for those willing to pursue it. Thompson's story demonstrates both the possibilities and the challenges inherent in American life, the ways in which our society can both enable and constrain individual achievement.

For readers seeking practical guidance, Thompson's memoir offers numerous lessons about resilience, risk-taking, and personal growth. His approach to failure as "a description of an event" rather than a judgment on personal worth provides a framework for recovering from setbacks. His emphasis on process goals over outcome goals offers a sustainable approach to achievement that can weather the inevitable ups and downs of any ambitious life.

The memoir's final chapters, focusing on Thompson's current life and his reflections on the journey that brought him to this point, provide a sense of completion while acknowledging that the story continues. His continued curiosity, his plans for future adventures, and his commitment to sharing his experiences with others demonstrate that a life well-lived is not a destination but an ongoing process of growth and discovery.

In presenting this memoir to readers, we offer not just the story of one remarkable life, but a source of inspiration and practical wisdom for anyone seeking to live more fully, taking meaningful risks, and finding purpose in both success and failure. Thompson's journey reminds us that the most important adventures are often the ones that take us furthest from our comfort zones, and that the greatest achievements are often measured not in dollars or accolades, but in the courage to keep beginning again.

PROLOGUE

The dust was everywhere that summer of 1945, coating everything in the two-room house where I took my first breaths—the rough wooden table where my mother prepared our meager meals, the single window that looked out over the endless rows of cotton that stretched to the horizon, even the air itself, thick and gritty with the remnants of topsoil that had once supported farms in Oklahoma and Arkansas but now drifted like ghosts across the California landscape.

I was born into a world that John Steinbeck had already made famous, though I wouldn't understand that connection for many years. Weedpatch, California, was more than just a place on the map; it was a symbol of American resilience, a testament to the human capacity to endure and adapt in the face of overwhelming adversity. The families who had made their way to this corner of Kern County carried with them not just their few possessions, but the accumulated weight of generations of struggle and the unshakeable belief that somewhere, somehow, life could be better.

My parents, like thousands of others, had followed the promise of work westward along Highway 66, part of the great migration that would reshape both the American West and the American imagination. They came with calloused hands and empty pockets, with children to feed and dreams that had been battered but not broken by the economic catastrophe that had driven them from their homes. They came seeking not wealth or fame, but simply the chance to work, to provide for their families, and to build something lasting from the ruins of what they had lost.

The house where I spent my earliest years stood as a monument to both poverty and determination. With no electricity, no running water, and an outhouse that served as our bathroom, it represented the harsh realities that shaped the lives of Dust Bowl refugees. Yet it also represented something more: the willingness to start over, to make do with less, and to find dignity in the humblest circumstances. The lantern that provided our evening light cast shadows that danced across walls that had heard countless stories of hardship and hope, of families torn apart by economic forces beyond their control and slowly, painstakingly, rebuilt through sheer force of will.

My mother's family had sold everything they owned in Arkansas—their farm animals, their tools, their furniture—to buy the broken-down truck that carried them west. My uncle Ed held a lantern on the front fender to light the way during night driving, since the truck had no headlights. They were part of a river of humanity flowing toward what they hoped would be a promised land, carrying with them the accumulated wisdom of generations of farmers and the desperate hope that their children might have opportunities they themselves had never known.

The community that grew up around Weedpatch was unlike anything that had existed before in American history. It was a place where traditional social hierarchies had been flattened by shared adversity, where a family's worth was measured not by their past achievements but by their willingness to work and their commitment to helping their neighbors survive. The school that the community built with their own hands, using donated materials and volunteer labor, became a symbol of their determination to ensure that their children would have chances they themselves had been denied.

In this environment, I learned my first lessons about resilience, about the difference between poverty and hopelessness, and about the power of community to sustain individuals through the darkest times. I watched my parents work from dawn to dusk in the fields, their hands bleeding from the cotton bolls, their backs aching from the constant bending and lifting, yet never losing their belief that their sacrifices would create opportunities for their children.

The Pentecostal church that served as the spiritual center of our community provided more than religious instruction; it offered a framework for understanding suffering and hope, for making sense of lives that seemed to be shaped by forces beyond human control. The emotional intensity of the services, with their emphasis on personal transformation and divine intervention, reflected the psychological needs of people who had lost everything material but refused to surrender their faith in the possibility of redemption.

As a child, I absorbed these lessons without fully understanding their significance. I learned to make toys from discarded materials, to find entertainment in the simplest pleasures, and to view challenges as puzzles to be solved rather than obstacles to be feared. The alarm clock that my mother gave me to disassemble when I was four years old became my first lesson in curiosity and experimentation, teaching me that understanding how things work the first step is toward making them work better.

The swimming pool that our community built—the first in Kern County—represented more than just a recreational facility. It symbolized our collective belief that we deserved the same amenities as more prosperous communities, and our willingness to work together to create them. The fact that I nearly drowned in that pool during my first attempt to learn swimming became an early lesson in the importance of preparation and the dangers of overconfidence.

The agricultural work that defined our community's economic life provided its own education. In the fields, I learned about the relationship between effort and reward, about the importance of persistence in the face of monotonous tasks, and about the dignity that comes from contributing to something larger than oneself. The cycles of planting and harvesting that governed our lives taught me about patience, about the long-term thinking required for any meaningful achievement, and about the ways in which individual success depends on collective effort.

The discrimination that our community faced by established California residents added another layer to my early education. The signs that read "No Okies" and the violence that sometimes-greeted families seeking work or housing taught me about the arbitrary nature of social hierarchies and the importance of judging people by their character rather than their circumstances. These experiences planted seeds of empathy and understanding that would influence my approach to business and relationships throughout my life.

The stories that circulated through our community—tales of families who had made good, of children who had gone to college, of businesses started with nothing but determination and hard work—provided the mythology that sustained our collective hope. These stories taught me that transformation was possible, that circumstances could be changed through effort and intelligence, and that the American Dream, however battered and complicated, remained within reach for those willing to pursue it.

As I grew older and began to understand the broader context of our situation, I realized that I was part of a historical moment that would reshape American society. The Dust Bowl migration brought together people from diverse backgrounds and forced them to create new forms of community and cooperation. The children of this migration would go on to build the modern American West, to serve in World War II and Korea, and to participate in the economic boom that would define the latter half of the twentieth century.

The poverty of my childhood, rather than limiting my aspirations, seemed to expand them. Having experienced genuine want, I developed an appreciation for abundance that would serve me well in later business ventures. Having seen my parents work without complaint in the most difficult conditions, I learned that no honest work was beneath my dignity. Having witnessed the power of community cooperation in building our school and other facilities, I understood the importance of relationships and mutual support in achieving ambitious goals.

The education I received in the schools built by our community was unconventional but comprehensive. In addition to traditional academic subjects, we learned practical skills like construction, agriculture, and mechanics. We raised our own food, built our own facilities, and maintained our own equipment. This hands-on approach to learning taught me that knowledge without application is incomplete, and that the most valuable education comes from direct engagement with real-world challenges.

The teachers who chose to work in our schools, often at considerable personal and professional sacrifice, provided models of dedication and service that would influence my later decision to enter education myself. Their willingness to see potential in children who had been written off by mainstream society taught me about the transformative power of belief and high expectations.

The contrast between our community's internal solidarity and the hostility we faced from the outside world taught me about the complexity of American society, about the ways in which economic anxiety can fuel prejudice and discrimination, and about the importance of maintaining dignity and self-respect in the face of unfair treatment. These lessons would prove invaluable during later periods of my life when I faced business failures and personal setbacks.

As I prepare to tell the story of the journey that began in that dust-covered house in Weedpatch, I am struck by the realization that everything that followed—the military service, the business ventures, the adventures in distant lands, the multiple careers and retirements—was shaped by those early experiences of poverty, community, and hope. The resilience that enabled me to rebuild after losing millions in the 1980s recession was forged in the fields of Kern County. The curiosity that led me to build bamboo rafts in Fiji was first awakened by that alarm clock I disassembled as a four-year-old. The commitment to education that defined my later career was inspired by the teachers who saw potential in the children of Dust Bowl refugees.

This memoir is not just the story of one man's journey from poverty to success and back to purpose. It is also a testament to the enduring power of the values and lessons learned in America's most challenging circumstances. It is a reminder that our greatest strengths often emerge from our deepest struggles, and that the most meaningful achievements are often built on foundations of hardship and hope.

The dust has long since settled in Weedpatch, and the community that shaped my early years has been transformed by time and progress. But the lessons learned in that place and time continue to guide my steps, and the dreams that sustained my parents and their neighbors continue to inspire new generations of Americans seeking to build better lives for themselves and their children.

This is where the journey begins—in the dust and dreams of Depression-era California, among people who had lost everything but their determination to begin again. It is a story that belongs not just to me, but to all who have faced impossible odds and chosen to keep moving forward, one step at a time, toward whatever possibilities the future might hold.

Dallas W. Thompson, MA, MBA With Distinction, PhD – Engineer License #344256, General Engineering, Contract C35 - LATHING AND PLASTERING, or A - GENERAL ENGINEERING, B - GENERAL BUILDING, C29 – MASONRY, Masonry, and Stucco. Credentialed Single Subject: Science, General Education with Administrative Credential.

DEDICATION

Thanks to my wife, Connie Thompson, my best friend who has inspired and supported me and my son, Dallas Steven Thompson.

CONTENTS

Chapter 1-Early Life And Formative Years	1
Chapter 2-Challenges And Opportunities	7
Chapter 3-Weedpatch Camp	11
Chapter 4-The Climb—Pursuing A Dream	23
Chapter 5-Relationships	29
Chapter 6-Challenges And Triumphs	33
Chapter 7-First Retirement	39
Chapter 8-New Challenge	47
Chapter 9-Hostel With Bunk Beds.	51
Chapter 10 -Second Backpacking Adventure	61
Chapter 11-Fiji Islands – Consist Of Over 300 Islands.	67
Chapter 12-Sailing From Fiji To Australia On Raft	77
Chapter 13-Moved To Stockton, Retired	83
Chapter 14 -Transformation And Triumph	89
Chapter 15-After Four Retirements-Both	95
Epilogue	99
The Process Of Writing A Book	107
An Example Of Writing A Children's Book	161

CHAPTER 1

EARLY LIFE AND FORMATIVE YEARS

In this autobiography, join me in my extraordinary journey in life, doing it rather than wishing I had done it. Born into the dust-choked humble surroundings of Bakersfield, California, the eldest of three. I have one sister, Rachel Regnart, and one living brother, George Thompson, and one deceased brother, Mark.

Headed to California: the "Land of Milk and Honey."

My mother's family jammed everything they owned into a car like this. Broke, hungry, and bound for California. They journeyed westward as refugees of the Great Depression.

My mother's family jammed everything they owned into this car. They were broke, hungry, and on their way to California.

Our home was a two-room house with an outhouse (outdoor toilet) above a hole in the ground. It had no utilities, and the lantern gave a warm night glow. It was in a community called Lamont, a rural enclave where our poverty-stricken family lived near Bakersfield and Weedpatch, California. The cycles of agriculture dictated their actions.

Poverty was our constant companion. From an early age, my family worked in the fields, hand-picking cotton and potatoes under the relentless sun. These early experiences instilled a work ethic and a desperation that would become the bedrock of my future endeavors.

Financial constraints were a constant companion in high school. I earned money from various jobs, such as mowing lawns with a push lawn mower for fifty cents to earn lunch money. I bartered for my first bicycle parts with determination. Imagine my sense of accomplishment in assembling the parts to build something I could ride. Despite lacking tires, it symbolizes my resourcefulness and resolve to overcome challenges. Imagine my surprise when I learned to ride my bicycle backwards. No one else could do it.

It was fun learning and trying something new. Despite having no tires on my rims, my bicycle could go faster than my friends' bikes. I eventually installed used tires for a smoother and softer ride.

Lunches often consisted of non-refrigerated bologna sandwiches with mayonnaise, carefully packed in a brown paper sack for the next day. Sometimes in high school, buying food like the rest of the students was a special event where savoring and enjoying eating each bite of a five-cent Big Hunk candy bar and a ten-cent bag of popcorn, with water serving as a reliable means to stave off hunger, made me feel like I had a wonderful lunch. Purchasing a cafeteria lunch, which cost 25 cents, was a rare pleasure.

By the age of thirty-three, my financial situation had improved to the point that my investment income was sufficient, making employment unnecessary. Work was not a requirement. This unexpected achievement brought a unique set of challenges. People often use their work as their identity. When one does not work, who are you? One of the many philosophical inquiries was, "What is the purpose of life?" Who am I? What are my goals in life? I grappled with the complexities of surpassing one's ambitions. I discovered and experienced the phenomenon of overachievement. It was as disorienting as underachievement. Underachievement was viewed as a failure. The definition of overachievement had to be explored, and I had to decide how the term was integrated into my life. What is success, and how did this idea assimilate within my life? The notions transformed into a vivid tapestry woven from the threads of challenges and struggles to adapt, do it, and learn daily. Success is subject to one's perspective. My success was defined as looking back from the mirror of life and loving the person looking back, despite the imperfections. Success is unconditional love of oneself.

My first retirement was after being a Honda dealer. My second retirement was after buying and selling apartments and being a real estate broker.

After these different career choices, the excitement and need for adventure led me to explore Europe. A Eurail ticket allows unlimited train rides. In Berlin, Germany, in 1989, I chipped away at the Berlin Wall with a hammer, celebrating the discovery of personal freedom as East Berliners rejoiced in their newfound liberty. The Berlin Wall has many meanings. For me, the Berlin Wall symbolized the harshness of human nature, the significance of liberty, and the vitality of democracy.

Sleeping beside electric eels on a flat rock in the middle of the stream was a surreal experience in the Cook Islands. The eight hours spent wading and jumping over waterfalls was not reassuring. It was not possible to get out of the stream. Waiting for dawn to arrive was a long night. At the time, the excitement and the experience of exploring were not relevant. One learns to be resilient. I left to explore Fiji.

The need for exploration and to find challenges led me to embark on an ambitious project in Fiji to build a 50-foot bamboo raft, known locally as a BiliBili. Teaming up with Rob, the nephew of Prime Minister Sitiveni Rabuka, our goal was to sail to the iconic Sydney Opera House in Australia. This endeavor aimed to revive traditional Fijian navigation methods, using celestial cues and bamboo rafts for ocean voyages.

This book isn't a manual on achieving success but a chronicle of my journey—a testament to the lessons learned and the experiences that have shaped me. As a committed lifelong learner, each day offers an opportunity for growth and development. By sharing my journey, I aspire to inspire others to pursue their paths of discovery. This book is about overcoming challenges and creating opportunities.

My journey of discovery and learning to just do it rather than talking about doing it has woven my threads of life experiences into a colorful tapestry of many colors. The process of learning to be an entrepreneur, mitigating the risks to ensure maximum financial gain, mirrors my philosophical point of view of life. Wealth unraveled existential questions: Who am I without work? What defines success? The answers lie not in balance sheets but in the mirror. Unconditional self-love.

CHAPTER 2

CHALLENGES AND OPPORTUNITIES

My early childhood was an adventure of making my own toys. I learned how to disassemble objects around me and reassemble them through trial and error, driven by necessity. An example of my curiosity is when, at the age of four years old, my mother gave me an alarm clock and set me in the middle of the floor to enable her to do household chores. In the meantime, my constant curiosity prompted me to find a bobby pin (a hairpin to hold hair in place) and use it as a screwdriver to unscrew and figure out how the clock worked. I had clock parts scattered all over the floor. My mother did not give me time to decide how to put the clock back together.

My curiosity has always motivated me to ask questions and seek understanding. Another early memory is in third grade, when we learned how to add four columns of numbers above each other. My classmates complained about how hard it was. We experimented with all possible combinations to determine the most challenging method for adding. Adding diagonally and straight across to figure out why it was difficult to add the numbers was all too easy. It seemed too simple to add as instructed. We had to memorize the timetable in the fourth grade. Every week, we added a new number. The first week, most of the students quickly understood that 1 X 1 = 1, 1 X 2 = 2, and so on until up to 1 X 12. The moment was just before recess. As soon as you master the new time number, you can go to recess. I needed only one session to review the new number timeline. I just remembered. Being the first one to go to recess was fun. Being first gave me the opportunity to choose which ball or game I wanted to play. Others recorded the time taken for their activities, such as during the first week and twice in the second week. The practice continued until they had learned up to their twelve-time tables. A few students had difficulty learning their timetables. They did not enjoy recess, since they never learned their timetables.

Being poor provided benefits. We had no television, nor a telephone. Reading a book every day provided a glimpse into worlds that were hard to imagine. Travel was fascinating. Having books to read was a challenge. The library was a mile walk each week. Five or six books were all that my arms could carry. Imagine my excitement when an old set of encyclopedias was found in a large box while walking from the library. Every page was studied and read. Reading was an ongoing learning experience. Learning was fun. Being poor was not experienced. My mother sewing my socks every day before school was just something she did. In the fifth grade, wearing my only pair of shoes in class, the teacher became annoyed by the flapping of my soles because they were worn. She called out, "Dallas, don't you have a better pair of shoes?" I replied, "no. " She then asked the class, "Does anyone have any spare shoes at home?" Some students raised their hands and replied, "Yes." She then asked them to "bring the shoes to school tomorrow."

The next day was like Christmas. There were multiple pairs of shoes and boots to select from. No one teased me or asked questions. It was just the way it was. All the students were children of the Dust Bowl famine refugees, which John Steinbeck's The Grapes of Wrath is deeply connected to the Dust Bowl, a period of severe drought and dust storms in the American Southwest during the 1930s.

The middle school was near Weedpatch, California where John Steinbeck met with Dorothy Lange and my relatives. My relatives thought they were making fun of them because they were taking pictures of the children playing in the muddy puddles. My relative took their camera away from them and stomped it into the mud. They were proud of who and what they were. They face daily challenges of discrimination. Some examples are when their vehicles stopped for gas near the California border, they were met by angry California people who had ax handles, hammers, and whatever else they could find to beat back the hungry, depression era refugees from the Oklahoma and Arkansas areas. The "Okies" were hungry and would work for any price. The locals resented these actions because the "Okies" would displace the California workers, and they would also work cheaper.

Hundreds of thousands of Okies traveled west along Route 66 to California's Central Valley, where they had heard there was work picking crops. But they found themselves facing stiff competition for jobs and discrimination from Californians who viewed them as undesirable and a threat to social stability. With few resources or choices, many migrants lived as squatters in camps along roads and stream banks. They had no running water and only tents, cars, or lean-tos for shelter. Tuberculosis spread through these camps, and child mortality was high.

California became the Promised Land to the "Okies." Blue skies, fertile soil, and work were the promise, so many loaded up their cars and jalopies for the long drive west. Handbills from growers needing help with harvesting enticed thousands. Those who made it across four states and two thousand miles through the Tehachapi Mountains of California appeared through the San Joaquin Valley.

During the Dust Bowl and World War II, Route 66 was used for migration and labor movements. It became a symbol of American culture and the road trip. became a symbol of American culture and the road trip.

But the Promised Land had overextended its promises. There was such a surplus of labor that growers could underpay the desperate field hands. With no money and no work, Okies slept wherever they could in the open. In the fertile land of California, some of them starved to death.

CHAPTER 3

WEEDPATCH CAMP

Life in the camp was a haven from a hostile world. Farmers forced migrants to work for near-slave wages and often used the police as a private force to deal with troublemakers who tried to organize for better conditions and pay.

Concerned about the squalid conditions in the squatters' camps, the federal government intervened to aid the migrants. The Works Progress Administration (WPA), a New Deal agency, constructed Arvin Federal Camp, near the town of Weedpatch, California, in 1935. With running water for showers, bathrooms, and laundry rooms, and wood platforms chosen for tents, the facility was a step up from squatters' camps.

Some Okie children faced significant prejudice while trying to obtain an education. During that period, the police officers received orders to physically assault the Okie families entering their state.

There had even been a mob headed by the sheriff that burned down another Okie migrant camp. People fueled by hatred and prejudice wanted to drive them out of California. But they had nowhere else to go.

They were treated as poorly as non-citizens and non-whites—all poor billboards in Oklahoma, Arkansas, and Texas carried news of the promise of work, food, and sunshine in California. For many, the opportunity was their only choice—to move to California. Most took Highway 66 to Highway 99, which led to Lamont, Arvin, Weedpatch, Delano, Tulare, Visalia, and Bakersfield. Since many came from Oklahoma, they became known as the "Okies."

These people replaced the Mexican farmworkers, who had been forced to return to Mexico the previous year. Their return was because the citizens of the United States were fearful that the Mexicans were taking jobs needed by American citizens during the Great Depression. Millions of the Okies came, but there were not enough jobs or places to live for them all. Most lived in poverty under poor conditions, became sick, and tragically died. They migrated in search of a better life than the one they abandoned. It is interesting to note that the Okies have assimilated into society, and most of them have become prosperous. My mother became a millionaire. She purchased and sold apartments and hotels.

Leo Hart, a teacher, visited Weedpatch Camp, took off his shoes, tie, and coat, and played catch with the children. Despite their rough manners and etiquette, he found them to be "ordinary kids."

He became Kern County Superintendent of Schools in April 1949, and after trying to integrate the Okie kids into the regular schools, he decided to build the Okies as a school of their own. This school was at no cost to Kern County, so he got swift permission to do so. A poor environment provided the motivation to make money. The "Okies" found various areas to stay while they worked in the fields.

__Weedpatch, a community of Okies, hungry and wanting to work.__

My mother's family sold their farm animals in Arkansas and traded their one cow for a pickup truck that had no headlights. My uncle, Ed, would hold a lantern on the right front fender to enable Grandpa to drive at night. Initially, my relatives resided near the canals due to the availability of boiled water for washing and drinking. The local school district did not want the "Okies'" students. The term "Okie" originated as a shorthand way to refer to someone from Oklahoma. However, it evolved into a derogatory term during the Great Depression and Dust Bowl era when migrants from Oklahoma and surrounding states, facing hardship and labeled as such by Californians, migrated to California seeking better opportunities.

They had a peculiar smell, spoke in a humorous manner, and possessed animal characteristics. The "Okies" built their own school. They named it Vineland. My mother graduated from this school. Later they built a middle school called Sunset School. Sunset School had the first swimming pool. The students with parental supervision dug the swimming pool by using shovels.

The Vineland School District encompasses thirty-three square miles in rural/agricultural southeast Kern County and is composed of two schools: Vineland School, which serves students in grades kindergarten through fourth grade, and Sunset School, which serves students in grades five through eight.

The Vineland School District was formed on May 9, 1890, as a one-school district, and during its first year of operation had an average daily attendance of fourteen students. Enrollment in the district remained modest until after 1920, when the beginnings of large-scale agricultural development attracted migrant farm workers to the area. By the 1929-1930 school year, the average daily attendance in the district was 225 students. Ten years later, the average daily attendance rose to 309 students.

I almost drowned in this pool. The pool had no electrical pumps to circulate the water. Every week, they drained the water to the football field and refilled it with Purex bleach to sanitize the pool. The pool had a deep end that was separated from the shallow end by a rope. The diving board was the best part.

The location being referred to is the field adjacent to the camp. The school was established with two condemned buildings that had stood in the field for years, along with fifty poorly clad and undernourished students. Leo began visiting universities and seeking teachers with a passion for teaching. He warned them all that they would begin teaching at the most basic levels.

Then, Leo asked for donations for everything from lumber, building supplies, and tools to farm animals, books, typewriters, and clothing. Teachers might teach history and math in the morning and then teach construction "hands-on" while the kids helped build their own school. Some teachers taught part of the day and then helped in the cafeteria. A teacher who taught chemistry, typing, and stenography also showed the girls how to make their own face cream and soaps, and they also teach hygiene practices.

Leo became a beggar of everything so that taxpayers could not complain about the Okie school. Donations began to pour in as resolute, caring people caught the spirit. As the school progressed, it began to prepare lunches using its own raised and grown food. Families took part in helping in the fields so that they could be fed. In addition to learning basic subjects, kids received training in construction, agriculture, butchering, office tasks, and a variety of other skills.

The school had agriculture classes to encourage students to grow their food, such as cattle, hogs, and vegetables. Later my relatives congregated around an area called "Weedpatch."

Sadly, there were still occasional attacks of hatred, such as arson and dead animals dumped at school, but the evolution of the Okies at Weedpatch School was truly remarkable. Gradually, word spread that some of the best teachers in the country, the best chemistry equipment, and the best course in auto mechanics were at the Okie school.

Breakfast was sold for one cent and lunch for two cents with all the ingredients prepared, grown, and raised at the school. The school especially became known for its total lack of disciplinary problems.

My favorite thing to do was to grow turnips! I enjoyed eating them. I acquired practical farming skills. I learned how to prune trees, castrate pigs, dig ditches, feed farm animals, start siphon pipe irrigation, and many more skills.

Additionally, you could learn basic airplane skills using a Link trainer and real airplanes.

Everyone picked cotton.

Because of the inconsistency in farm work for the migrants, they were unable to secure housing and faced a life of homelessness. Most would live on the side of the road or in ditch banks and others would build homes from the materials available, such as packing crates. These homes were coined "Migratory Jungles." Although having a home in a labor camp is an improvement over living in the "Migratory Jungles," it still presents its own set of problems. Starvation, unsanitary living conditions, and a lack of access to affordable medical services were issues that plagued residents at the Arvin Federal Government Camp. Outbreaks of smallpox, tuberculosis, malaria, and pneumonia were common in the camps. The Okies could not afford to see the doctors. The Pentecostal religion did not believe in seeing doctors. "Trust in God."

My mother used a 12-foot-long sack to make more money. Fun riding on top of the sack!

Weedpatch still exists. It is fourteen miles Southeast of Bakersfield, California. The one church was colorful. My father was flirting with my mother, waiting outside for church to dismiss, when a young boy came outside to use the outhouse. My father, looking to have fun, stripped this young man of his clothes. The police summoned my father, who then fled across the backyards. One of the backyards had a clothesline.

My father did a quick backflip when his neck hit the clothesline and had to explain to the friendly police why he chose to do what he did. He did not do that again.

My father became converted to the Pentecostal religion. It was a drastic change from a fist-fighting, beer drinking, smoking, cussing individual to an emotional driven religion that interpreted the bible literally. No movies, no television, long sleeves, and ten percent tithes paid to the church.

During this period, the Okies' preferred religion was Pentecostal. The church was characterized by loud singing, exuberance, and occasional outbursts of laughter. The sermons were fiery. For example, "You were held over the fires of hell, with every breath you took potentially being your last." They were good, uneducated people. I was one of the first to get a college education. I never joined the church. It was an emotionally based viewpoint.

Weedpatch Camp built the school. Later they built the first swimming pool in Kern County. I almost drowned in this swimming pool in the fifth grade. My father did not allow me to swim with girls. He considered them "half naked." Despite my father forbidding me, I borrowed a pair of cut-off Levis and persuaded my friend Pedro to jump off the diving board and learn how to swim.

My "research" consisted of asking my friends how they learned to swim. All of them replied, "Our brothers threw us into the Kern River." I expected to learn to swim the same way. My friend jumped first and dog-paddled to the rope. My friend Pedro's success swimming to the rope that separated the deep end from the eight-foot-deep end gave me the confidence to dive off the board. I jumped and pushed up from the bottom three times. The third time, I gulped for air and got choked. The next time I came up, I grabbed a passing swimmer and missed. I swam like a rock.

The last thing I remembered was floating back down to the bottom with the thought, "What if I drown? So what?" as my reply. I was not afraid to die. The next thing I knew was staring up from the swimming pool deck, looking up at the lifeguard, Mr. Hamstreet and all my friends staring down at me.

The boys' and girls' changing room had no roof. There was no pool filter equipment. Purex was used to sanitize the pool with once-per-week drainage to the football field. Most boys wore cut-off pants for their bathing suits. The girls wore regular swimsuits.

Sunset swimming pool. First school pool in the county.

In May 1949, Mr. Bancroft leased a ten-acre site of land for ten dollars from the federal government next to the campground. He found the best and most resolute teachers from California state universities and colleges and got the material to build the school with donated supplies. Clothing and shoes came from the Salvation Army, and many others donated slightly used paint and a huge used water heater. Adults and fifty children from

The principal of the school, Pete Bancroft, bought a C-47 plane from military surplus for $200 for the children to learn aircraft mechanics. They had a railroad car for a workshop. School started in the fall of 1940, and by the spring of 1941, the school had become completely self-sufficient with potatoes, vegetables, milk, eggs, and beef, which they raised themselves. The community built the school on a cash basis. Mr. Bancroft approached local companies to sponsor the school. Many locals donated what they could. The locals built a school for students rejected by the local school district. Bakersfield Unified School District did not want these students.

They smelled foul and talked funny.

The schools flourished. The local school district, Bakersfield Unified School District, wanted to annex them. Vineland and Sunset School refused. The government donated military surplus planes, trainers and parts for hands-on learning. We used one of the planes for classroom purposes. The classroom felt awkward due to the tilt of the C-47 plane. It was a C-47.

C-47 used as a classroom.

Life was boring for others. I had to go to church every other night and twice on Sundays. During the revival at the church, services were held every night and twice on Sundays. I hated church.

Church was the focal point of the community. The Okie people were searching for a meaning in life. The Pentecostal church was an emotional and physical religion where the saints would shout, speak in an unknown tongue, roll on the sawdust floor, and run up and down the aisle.

Many times, the preacher would point at me and tell me, "You are held over the fires of hell by a single thread, and your next breath could be your last." I never joined the church.

We made our toys. I had a champion slingshot that was accurate. Pieces of an innertube and a shoe tongue for the rock with a forked tree limb for the handle were used. I used string to tie the innertube to the handle, with holes cut into the leather for the shoe tongue to hold the rocks.

A life lesson I learned when I was around nine years old was the value of being goal-oriented. My cousin, Jack Rose, challenged me to see who could walk the furthest across a vacant field barefoot. It was covered with "goatheads," a sticker that was everywhere. The absence of shoes left our feet calloused. We only wore shoes to church and to school.

Goatheads, AKA, "stickers"

Jack, who is six months older than I, tiptoed gingerly and got stuck with stickers at every step. He did not go far. I ran across the field and won! I learned to focus on the outcome, not on the process. When the stickers penetrated my foot, I did not feel them. Jack felt every sticker puncturing his feet.

I received many whippings with a belt for my actions in church. My father believed the biblical verse that corresponds to "spare the rod, spoil the child" in Proverbs 13:24: "Whoever spares the rod hates their children, but the one who loves their children is careful to discipline them." This verse emphasizes the importance of discipline. My upbringing was unspoiled. The benefits of being raised by a strict father have taught me the value of obeying orders from political entities, including cities, counties, states, and the federal government. It also taught me to be true to myself. To not be influenced by others.

My father at an early age taught me a valuable lesson on how to be creative. After I told my father I was bored, he made me dig a hole, write on a piece of paper, and cover it up. I was never bored after that experience. I learned to find things to do. I learned how to have a life of discovery. I had a strictly demanding father. I was unable to ask why. I had to obey my elders and my father.

Baptism time. People in the canal being "Saved."

CHAPTER 4

THE CLIMB – PURSUING A DREAM

During my eighth grade, during an IQ test, the psychologist gave me the impression he was wasting his time assessing me because I was not taking the test seriously. I answered the questions as quickly as he could ask them. His confusion was that the testing was too easy for me. Notwithstanding, state testing was a bore. It did not make sense to me to try to do well on a test that did not help me. The state-mandated test scoring sheets, where you had to pencil in a square for an answer, created patterns during state testing. Imagine the psychologist's surprise when my test results were the highest, exceeding the rich students' scores. At my eighth-grade graduation, my picture was displayed by a projector on the gym wall before school as a future scientist wearing a white uniform jacket. Science was fun. After retiring as a businessperson, teaching science was one of my most enjoyable careers as an adult.

My high school experience was boring. I could not join any social clubs or activities. My parents considered going to church the most important thing to do. Schools were perceived as both worldly and anti-Christ. If a "C" was obtained, my parents were happy. I would take the tests, receive "A's," and get "F's" for not doing my homework to get my desired "C." I did not take college classes. Education was not relevant. Additionally, who would want to take classes that required studying? Coaches constantly asked me to "go out for sports." I was embarrassed to tell them I could not play sports after school. My father believed, "Pride goeth before a fall." The phrase is a common idiom, meaning that excessive pride or arrogance often leads to failure or downfall, and it is a shortened version of the biblical proverb "Pride goeth before destruction, and a haughty spirit before a fall" (Proverbs 16:18). He was a preacher. He was strict. My mother played the piano.

Weedpatch Supermarket, now

Working at Weedpatch Supermarket at 16 years old gave me the chance to understand the value of personal relationships. Starting as a "box boy," the money was great. A box boy used cardboard boxes that the groceries came in, and when they were empty, we put groceries that the customer had bought into the empty boxes. I worked my way up from initially sorting pop bottles to learning how to sack ten-pound potatoes, shuck onions, stock produce, restock the delicatessen, stock beer and wine, and stock groceries; eventually, I became a cash register operator.

My first car. A Triumph TR3 - The car was powered by a 1991 cc straight-4 OHV engine which initially produced 95 bhp.

By the time I reached my senior year, I had purchased a new 1963 Chevrolet Impala. I earned more than my father in my senior year of high school. My focus was on work, not school. The five years of greeting people and providing a service in the grocery business was excellent training.

I left home when I was seventeen. My father told me when I left, "That door swings one way." This statement put a steel rod into my backbone. I would never come back home to live. I graduated at the age of seventeen.

A portable well repair rig, also known as a "bull-shitter rig."

Wanting more, I joined the United States Air Force. During basic training, when I was called into the drill sergeant's flight office and told, "At ease," I expected the worst. He asked me if I wanted to be in charge when he was absent. I told him no. I knew that I should never volunteer while serving in the military! He explained I could stay up as late as I wanted, and I would get to lead the men marching. I asked why he wanted me to be the leader. He said, "Because I have watched you when I call fire drills, and the men follow you and do what you tell them."

I learned quickly to give out orders and to herd cats. The basic airman was young, scared, and often did things without thinking. Herding cats is an analogy. The troops anticipated receiving a stern lecture. Quickly, we became a unit doing activities as one, each supporting the other—our team's effort rewarded success in all our endeavors.

Upon completing basic training, we got our orders while standing in formation. Imagine learning my assignment was for a year at Lackland Air Force Base in Crypto School. The U.S. Air Force's cryptologic training, often called "crypto school," prepares airmen for careers in intelligence analysis, focusing on analyzing encrypted communications and signals intelligence. I had no idea what this course was. Crypto School was at the edge of the base. It was a two-story building with no windows. A career USAF sergeant, who had reenlisted and owned a brand-new Avanti sports car, marched us to and from school. I learned he was a spy. His name was Beckenhauf. The government followed him for two years to determine what he wanted to know and to whom he was reporting. In Washington, C., he met a Russian "friend" at a bowling alley. Beckenhauf told his "new best friend" he would apply to re-enlist in the Air Force.

The new friend suggested he apply for the Crypto School, a top-secret facility. It was suspected this new friend was either a double agent or a government employee trained to spot security breaches or lapses. The government made sure he received everything he asked for. The base commander was told to give him off-base passes whenever requested. No one knew he was a spy at this time. He was an unusual example of a US citizen selling US secrets who continually asked the Russian government for more money and more information. We were trained to think the opposite.

The "bad guys" would try to get information and offer favors, benefits, or money—anything that you would want. Another example was John Walker's (US Navy) Espionage episode, in which he and his family sold our secrets items to the Russians.

Davis Monthan Air Force Base, Tucson, Arizona

CHAPTER 5

RELATIONSHIPS

Getting married at 20 years old while in basic training in the United States Air Force provided benefits. There was no constant harassment from others. The absence of inspections allowed for greater independence. The wedding was simple at the base chapel, with two witnesses. I made $175 per month. My wife worked at Lubey's, a San Antonio, Texas restaurant, and earned around $400 per month. Rent was $150 per month. My wife would get her meals free, and mine would be at half price. We would switch plates.

After crypto school, I received instructions to report to the Davis-Monthan Air Force Base in Tucson, Arizona. Tucson had nuclear-tipped missiles surrounding the city.

Being assigned to the Strategic Air Command system. The Strategic Air Command (SAC) was a United States Department of Defense command responsible for strategic air forces, primarily bombers and missiles capable of nuclear delivery. It played a crucial role in the Cold War as a nuclear deterrent against the Soviet Union.

This assignment needed a "Top Secret Crypto" and, in addition, a "Human Reliability" clearance. The human reliability clearance was because in a certain area, there were wires that could be connected that would bypass all the safety procedures and fire a nuclear-tipped missile. The government declared these areas as "two-man" zones. How would we enforce this requirement?

The mid-1980s saw the activation of the infamous Titan II nuclear-tipped missiles, which ringed Tucson and pointed at the USSR for 20 years.

Titan nuclear-tipped missiles surrounding Tucson, Arizona

The 390th Strategic Missile Wing, headquartered at Davis-Monthan AFB, Tucson, was active from 1962 to 1984 and commanded the 18 sites in Southern Arizona. The Reagan Administration decided to retire the missiles by 1987. Demolition crews decommissioned the silos by imploding them and sealing access points with concrete. My duty station required me to return to Crypto School at Lackland Air Force Base for additional training. While there, being awakened in the middle of the night, I was given orders to report at once to my duty station for a classified overseas assignment. The classified assignment was to the Joint Chiefs of Staff, Far East Command in Kunia, Hawaii, near Wheeler Airfield and Schofield Barracks.

Kunia facility was classified and to not be easily noticed. Marine guard hut, to the left.

Moving to Hawaii requires planning. The USAF did not pay for my wife's transportation or expenses. We transported our belongings via the United States mail, which resulted in some damage during transit. Meeting her on my Kawasaki 120 CC motorcycle at the airport provided a windblown experience.

My wife carried a garbage can with our stuff when we moved, and we used a motorcycle. The process took two trips. At the new apartment, we had no furniture. We made a bed by folding a used carpet. A radar crate served as our dining table. Our amusement was watching the gecko lizards walk on the walls and ceilings.

The number of pop bottles we picked up and sold at the supermarket often determined our meals. I acquired the valuable lesson of not stealing pineapples from the pineapple fields through hard experience. Riding my motorcycle with the pineapple under my shirt was painful, pricked with the pointed leaves that hurt. The pineapple tasted delicious with rice.

Initially, we cooked on an iron turned upside down. We did not have gas to cook with.

Keeping a savings account was a fantastic financial cushion. We never had less than $5,000 in savings. When we left Hawaii, I discovered hundreds of dollar bills hidden in my drawers!

CHAPTER 6

CHALLENGES AND TRIUMPHS

Stationed at Kunia "Tunnel" Field Station (KFS) in a three-story underground facility, which was initially designed as a protected Army/Navy facility for aircraft assembly, located near Wheeler Army Airfield and Schofield Barracks in Hawaii, and now used by the National Security Agency. The Hawaii Cryptologic Center (HCC) or NSA Hawaii is a U.S. National Security Agency (NSA) Central Security Service (CSS) facility located near Wahiawa on the island of Oahu, Hawaii.

The center focuses on signals intelligence intercepts from Asia and conducts cybersecurity and cyberwarfare operations. In May 2013, a worker at this facility, Edward Snowden, took thousands of classified documents and provided them to the press, revealing the existence of several top-secret NSA mass surveillance programs.

No one could recognize the facility. It is in a canyon with a pineapple field above. There was a marine hut at the entrance of the tunnel. The entrance was a tunnel about a quarter mile long with a large curve. The curve was to deflect a bomb blast. Inside was another personnel door that had positive air pressure. Upon entering, the only areas visible were corridors. One approached their duty station and rang a buzzer.

Upon recognizing you from the TV monitor, personnel inside would buzz you in. We were unaware of what lay behind the other doors. People did not talk to each other.

My assignment was with the Joint Chiefs of Staff—Far East. They had a classified mission that required me to report my estimated time of arrival (ETA) when off duty on an hourly basis. The difference between the "good guys" and the "bad guys" was unknown. The acceptable behavior was not to question orders but to do as instructed. My childhood of being told what to do and not to question orders made me perfect for this job. One cannot talk about what they did in the classified arena. It was stressful. I have PTSD because of this experience.

While in this stressful environment, after completing a battery test at Schofield Barracks, US Army, Hawaii, and being awarded the maximum testing credits from Chaminade University of Honolulu, I was allowed credits toward a bachelor's degree. Interestingly, there were enough electronic courses to qualify for an electrical engineering degree. I decided to major in business because it gave me a broader perspective. By attending the University of Hawaii and Chaminade University of Honolulu simultaneously, I could graduate within fifteen months of starting the process and completing it with a bachelor's degree. It was stressful. Feeling like you had a hangover during this time was normal. The timing was critical. Rushing from work required me to change from my military uniform to civilian clothes while driving from Kunia to Chaminade University of Honolulu, Hawaii. Getting to the University of Hawaii for my subsequent classes was always challenging because it is in a different part of Honolulu.

The Joint Chiefs of Staff-Far East unit assigned me to the position of off-duty education officer. This unit discharged me to a civilian status, committing me to the Air Force on a long-term reserve basis.

Given that I had worked for Union Oil Company prior to my time in the USAF, Union Oil agreed to hire me. Upon passing the required Federal Communications Commission Second Class License, I qualified to work in the Communication Department for the installation, adjustment, and repair of two-way radio gear.

I obtained a first-class license, enabling me to oversee logs, frequencies, and broadcast practices. The job challenges became routine in the same problem-solving process, leading to a transfer to the accounting department.

My department was in the Refining and Marketing Division. My main responsibility was to monitor budgets for gas station construction. Closing the books and ensuring that each account was perfectly balanced was my biggest challenge. During this time, comptometers were used. A comptometer is a mechanical calculator, specifically an adding machine, which was widely used from the late 19th century to the mid-1970s. While initially designed for addition, comptometers could also perform subtraction, multiplication, and division. Daily, I would ask for more work. I had side chores to keep me busy.

I took on a role as a "bookkeeper" at Beeler Wilson Honda in Lamont, California. Lamont is a small rural community of around 7,000 citizens.

Beeler Wilson meeting Mr. Honda. My first mentor.

Beeler Wilson was a friend I knew in the Pentecostal church. He was the richest man I knew and trusted. He was a deacon in the church. He had an innate sense of being an outstanding salesperson from the "old school." He could add quicker in his head than I could on a ten-key. He kept asking me to "wait on these people." My job was to pay the bills and not wait on customers. I resented acting as a salesperson. Eventually, my sales ability was an outstanding success in assisting people in making their choices to purchase a Honda.

My sales success resulted in my promotion to the general manager position. The Honda dealership prospered. After three years as the general manager at Beeler Wilson Honda, ownership became a possibility. As the owner, I learned how to act as the "spokesperson" in the advertisement campaigns. I was on the television once per day and on the radio five times per day.

By working 12-hour days, seven days a week, and employing aggressive marketing through radio, television, and newspapers, the dealership achieved the highest sales volume of any Honda dealership in California. Honda awarded me a two-week, all-expenses-paid trip to Europe for being the highest-volume dealer in California. The most valuable tool I learned was how important personal relationships were to close the sale.

Although being a salesperson was not my first desire, I learned everyone is a salesperson. At birth we advertise our need for food by crying. Every day we advertise our needs and wants. I learned a good "closing" sales approach was to never lie and to simply identify their wants and weave a fabric of them enjoying the benefits of buying a Honda. This bedrock of my discovered reality provided benefits in everything that I do. We enjoyed the challenges as they transformed into benefits for all participants. The buyer was key to the team's effort to meet the needs of the public, employees, and customers.

CHAPTER 7

FIRST RETIREMENT

My first retirement was at the age of thirty-three. After being a top-notch Honda dealership for seven years, the challenge was gone. Working for seven years, seven days a week, 10 to 12 hours per day had burned me out. I had reached my limit. Retirement was a new idea and concept. My need for more money was satisfied. Retirement was simple for me. Retirement was to sit and not do anything. Being in demand for multiple tasks had become a chore.

Having more money than I dreamed of provided me with the opportunity to reassess who I am and what I am. The philosophical question is, "What is the purpose of life? "Who am I?" was now my challenge. I had ample income from buying and selling apartments in addition to the Honda dealership. The Honda dealership taught me the art of buying cheap and selling high. Initially, my accountant surprised me by asking, "How does it feel to be a millionaire?" I responded with, "What?" I was surprised. The new label did not feel any different.

I had read "Turning $1,000 into a Million in Real Estate," a well-documented success story, most famously detailed in William Nickerson's book. The core principle involves a combination of leveraging credit, finding undervalued properties, and strategically managing investments over time. The author has revised the title to "How I Turned $1,000 into a Million in Real Estate in My Spare Time." It is available on Amazon. The book provided the needed tools and knowledge to begin my real estate apartment enterprise.

One example from the beginning of my apartment-buying process is a 12-unit apartment complex. The 12-unit apartment complex needed minor repairs and an upgrade in appearance. I installed a roof on one unit in the summer. It was 105 degrees in the shade in Bakersfield, California. I used a running sprinkler to cool me and the roof. The roof is still on 40 years later. As soon as you raise the rents, apartments are more valuable. Apartments are the same as other investments. The bottom-line gains are what generate value.

When utilizing the IRS Like-Kind Exchanges under IRC Section 1031, which permits the sale of business or investment property with a gain, you are required to pay tax on that gain at the time of sale.

IRC Section 1031 provides an exception and allows you to postpone paying tax on the gain if you reinvest the proceeds in similar property that costs more than what you currently have invested as part of a qualifying like-kind exchange. Gains deferred in a like-kind exchange under IRC Section 1031 are tax-deferred, but they are not tax-free. Wait—there is more—by continuously using this section of the tax code, one can defer paying capital gains tax. One simply exchanges your property for a like-kind or more expensive unit each time you sell it. By setting up a trust, you can pass it along to your heirs tax-free.

There are strict guidelines to follow. See your tax accountant. For example, owners of investment and business properties may qualify for a Section 1031 deferral. Individuals, C corporations, S corporations, partnerships (general or limited), limited liability companies, trusts, and any other tax-paying entity may set up an exchange of business or investment properties under Section 1031. This process generates giant returns.

Using William Nickerson's book as a guide, one can leverage their money for giant returns. In addition, applying a known tax advantage amplifies one's return on their investments.

The following is a detailed example of how to earn a significant return on investment, which some readers may prefer to skip to the * section, located four paragraphs later.

An example of this is investing 25% of the $300,000 sales price for the above-mentioned 12-unit apartment complex, which amounts to a down payment of $75,000. I sold the apartments two years later at a price of $420,000 minus the $50,000 improvements, after deducting my initial investment of $75,000, generated a profit of $295,000 before taxes and prior to accounting for cash flow from rental income. The above units created a positive cash flow of around $18,000 per year. I owned the apartments for two years, which resulted in an additional $36,000, bringing my total profit to $331,000. Remember, I would rather not pay taxes; therefore, I use the above 1031 IRS tax-deferred exchange.

No bank will pay over triple your return on your investment. The return does not include the positive cash flow from the rental minus the operating income. Tax considerations applied to my ordinary income have produced a losing investment. Instead of paying taxes, I end up deducting a loss from my taxable income! Your total gain or loss would reflect your specific tax bracket and income.

Sometimes, losing money can ultimately lead to making more money. Get a competent accountant. Avoiding taxes and evading taxes are two different things. Avoid overstepping the boundaries. Understanding and mastering tax laws and their application in real estate transactions offers additional avenues for income generation. Saving money is making money. An example is the depreciation of rental properties. Depreciation is the gradual decline in an asset's value due to wear and tear, age, and obsolescence. For rental properties, it creates a tax deduction that owners use to recover the cost of their investment over time. The IRS requires property owners to spread the deduction across what it considers the property's useful life, rather than allowing them to deduct the entire amount in the year they purchase the property.

Depreciation is a powerful tax-saving tool for property owners, as it reduces their taxable income and can generate substantial tax savings overall.

For example, by claiming depreciation on a property, the cost of buying or improving the rental property can be deducted from the taxable income, thus decreasing the amount of income subject to taxation and, in turn, lowering the tax liability for the property owner.

I sold my first 12-unit apartment complex and recorded in escrow my plan to transfer my equity into a 50-unit apartment complex. I used this equity, which yielded a total profit of $331,000 (25% of the purchase price), as a down payment for a 30-unit apartment complex that sold for $1,300,000. I repeated this exercise several times. Each time, the next apartment complex was pricier. We achieved significant financial gains without having to pay any taxes.

*Depending on the situation, real estate depreciation can result in hundreds of thousands or millions of dollars in tax savings per year for real estate investors. Consult your tax accountant. There are multiple ways to apply depreciation. One method is accelerated depreciation. This strategy returns more tax savings.

Considering the previous exercise and the multiplication of transactions, one can see a significant return on investments. We faced yet another challenge. I met Doctor Chandler while selling him multiple Hondas, and he became a customer. We became friends. He was following the above author William Nickerson's advice. He, too, wanted to diversify his real estate activities. He asked me to find lots to enable him to build houses. I found a 57-lot subdivision that was for sale. We met the seller, a local real estate developer, who was a binge drinker. Neither the doctor nor I drank. Imagine our challenge meeting the developer and accepting drinks while we negotiated our "best" deal on a paper napkin. We, the buyers, benefited from the sale.

The developer had agreed to function as our general contractor in building all fifty-seven houses for no added fee. I knew these terms would not last. I contacted a general contractor school and purchased their textbooks. I passed the general contractor's examination. I became the general contractor. I had gained enough experience rehabilitating apartments, which provided knowledge and awareness of the construction process.

An example of homes built in Bakersfield, California. Note the skylight.

After this, by studying construction engineering principles, a general engineering license was acquired that utilized specialized engineering knowledge and skill, including refineries, chemical plants, and similar industrial plants requiring specialized engineering knowledge and skill; powerhouses, power plants, and other utility plants and installations; land leveling and earthmoving projects; excavating, grading, trenching, paving, and surfacing. I now had a California A - General Engineering, #344256; B - General Building; C29—Masonry; and C35 - Lathing and Plastering license.

We built off-site and on-site improvements as well as obtained FHA approvals and financing. It was a momentous success. I became a real estate broker and hired a sales team. As a vertically integrated entity in the housing market, an efficient real estate enterprise was created. By buying land, rezoning it, and developing it to its highest and best use, one mitigates the unknowns and maximizes profits. Multiple markets were addressed, such as apartments, shopping centers, single-family dwellings, subdivisions, and land use.

To maximize profits, one must figure out the highest and best use of the land. It is cheaper to build on the outskirts of a town. After one has determined the highest and best use, one must decide what housing product would satisfy a need the public has. At the time, Bakersfield needed startup housing. Startup housing requires ideal financing with low down payments. The subdivision was approved by the Federal Housing Authority (FHA) and the Veteran Administration (VA). This process enabled rapid selling of the approved subdivision. The sales staff worked for me as their real estate broker.

All financial decisions require a feasibility study. A financial feasibility study is a detailed evaluation that assesses the economic viability of a proposed project or business venture. It involves analyzing various financial aspects, such as initial capital requirements, operating expenses, revenue projections, cash flow forecasts, profitability, and expected return on investment (ROI). The goal is to determine if the project is financially sound and can generate the desired financial returns.

There I was, at the pinnacle of success—and yet, I had never felt emptier. Retired again. Got a divorce. Single for 15 years. I learned what the experience was to overachieve again. My experience was "What is next?" I had to learn to enjoy the process and not be goal oriented. The simple task of looking into the mirror and deciding if it was going to be a good day or a difficult day gave me the confidence to enjoy serendipity. I have always been goal oriented. One must learn balance. I learned to love myself as is. Acceptance of oneself was learned. To love the one looking back in a mirror is a bonus.

CHAPTER 8

NEW CHALLENGE

The trip to Europe provided a contrast to not working all the time. The change of pace was a welcome relief. Landing in Paris, France, was a culture shock. Using the itinerary supplied by the Honda Motor Company, it was a busy schedule. Each night there was a different show with exotic performers. It was beyond my expectations.

This was my first experience seeing Las Vegas-style entertainment. It was exemplary among professionals. Examples of the highlights were visiting the Eiffel Tower, the Louvre Museum, and Notre-Dame Cathedral and enjoying a Seine River cruise. The Louvre was my favorite. It reminded me of the Smithsonian Institution Building in Washington, D.C. Like the Smithsonian Institute, there are multiple areas to experience at the Louvre. One should plan for at least a week to explore the Louvre. Exploring the Louvre offered valuable insights into historical perspectives.

The encounter with the Mona Lisa picture was amusing. A sign said, "Do Not Take a Picture." Later, I discovered that I had no film.

My experience exploring foreign cultures and old history inspired a better appreciation of history. During school, history was not relevant. The contributions of old, dead people did not seem important. The process of discovering ancient buildings began in Paris.

My experience of visiting Paris, which was limited to only the best restaurants and hotels, did not fully represent what the city is truly like. There was much more to explore and discover about the intricate tapestry of France, which includes its rich cultures and diverse geographical settings. Not only Paris, but Europe in general was my desired area to explore for the next three months. For example, when a visitor stays in Los Angeles, that city does not accurately represent what California is like. Paris and Los Angeles each have unique neighborhoods that offer different environments. The essence of Europe and all its facets needed to be explored.

My priority was my choice of sleeping accommodation. The first-class hotels were not representative of the regular people. The discovery of hostels while engaged in conversation while standing near the Arc de Triomphe with a young man who had a backpack and a bicycle that explained how he traveled and stayed in hostels.

What is a hostel? I asked. He explained that "hostels are a type of shared accommodation that helps your travel budget go further. But what you may not know is that the unique social nature of hostels will transform your trip." He used this expression to describe the hostel experience. "With a hostel, you get to pay half the price for twice the fun."

Wanting to experience serendipity, I traveled to Europe with an Eurail Pass. The Eurail Pass gives non-European citizens and residents the freedom to visit top destinations with one convenient pass. You can select either a Consecutive Pass or a Flexible Pass, which allows you to choose to use your travel days consecutively or to split them up based on your itinerary and needs. Instead of juggling multiple tickets, you can easily access all your connections with your Eurail Global Pass and enjoy stress-free boarding and travel.

Planning to backpack, I read all the available literature about it. I had no idea what "backpacking" meant. Backpacking is an adventure that blends hiking with backcountry camping. It lets you broaden your horizons beyond the car campground to enjoy a richer, more immersive outdoor experience.

A key distinction from day hiking is the size of your pack—your backpack (and you) must carry all of life's essentials on your back. Backpacking is a form of low-cost, independent travel, which often includes staying in inexpensive lodgings and carrying all necessary possessions in a backpack. Once considered a marginal form of travel undertaken only through necessity, it has become a mainstream form of tourism.

Hostel sleeping area. Both sexes slept in the same rooms.

It is interesting to note that in all the hostels I have stayed in, both in Europe and the South Pacific, there have never been any public displays of affection. Occasionally a female would be next to me showering; it was no big deal. Most of the public restrooms were unisex.

CHAPTER 9

HOSTEL WITH BUNK BEDS.

Enjoy meeting people. While this activity may not appeal to everyone, if it interests you, there is little to lose by giving it a try. From a simple "country boy background, this backpacking experience provided opportunities for expanding personal relationships. We recommend this activity to most college graduates.

An example of a personal experience was hitchhiking with a young man, around 22 years old, from Paris to Calais, France, on the beach. He had spent two years backpacking all over Europe. He had a guitar that was a catalyst to connecting with others. He never spent one night under the stars. Someone, somewhere, always provided a place to sleep.

He shared a statement that, for me, summed up a broad perspective on life. "Life is experiencing contrasts. You appreciate the lows in life when you have also experienced the highs. If you have experienced hunger, then being full becomes more meaningful and pleasurable. You can best appreciate the valleys from the tops of the mountains.

France was my first stop at the Charles De Gaulle Airport. Having no idea where I was going, I boarded a bus that said "Paris.

Imagine my concern when this young man convinced me to go with him from Paris to London for free. As he explained, you could hitchhike to the outskirts of Paris to catch a truck. Once a truck picked you up, you simply stayed in it all the way to London. We both had backpacks and stored our bicycles in Paris. There is a freeway that connects Paris to Calais. We were unaware of the prohibition of hitchhiking on the freeways. We found out when the police officer explained the rules to us and drove us back to the center of Paris. Reaching the freeway required multiple train rides and bus transfers. We had to start over on our journey to London. We decided to try again. Again, a police officer picked us up. This time, they checked our passports. This time, the return trip to Paris was to its outskirts.

I told the young man, "I was not hitchhiking anymore." By taking a bus to Calais and a ferry to England, I discovered a new country to explore. In this place, antiquated elements coexist with contemporary ones. You will find both the historic Tower of London and the modern Tate Modern art gallery. You can catch both the Bard's works and modern plays at Shakespeare's Globe and its accompanying Sam Wanamaker Playhouse. While Londoners continue to praise the power of tea, they also make room for Starbucks and Costa Coffees, as well as pressed juice. London, a current leader in everything from politics and banking to fashion and music, consistently stays ahead of the trends. We appreciated the contrast and enjoyed the differences. We explored all the adjacent countries. Guinness was tasty but not appreciated.

There was still more to discover, so we headed back to Paris and boarded the Eurail train, which provides first-class travel in night trains. From reclining seats to private sleeping cabins, travelers can select a travel option that meets their every need. wish. Save precious travel time by traveling from one destination to the next while you sleep. I visited every country while sleeping on the trains. Each country was distinct, and each one offered a contrast to my previous life experiences. The process was enjoyable.

Some of the benefits enjoyed were reduced stress and a boost of energy. Stepping away from daily routines allowed relaxation and rejuvenation, leading to decreased stress levels and increased vitality. My social and cultural enrichment was a pleasant surprise.

The benefits included fostering empathy and understanding. Interacting with people from diverse backgrounds cultivated empathy and a deeper appreciation for global diversity. My travels strengthened relationships that created lasting memories and improved communication across diverse cultures. Experiencing diverse cultures improved my mental health. The discovery of spending time near water bodies, known as "blue spaces," increased my happiness and reduced anxiety. The outdoor activities in natural settings motivated individuals to engage in physical activities like swimming.

After ninety days of traveling in Europe without any agendas, I found the experience to be great; however, I was also ready to embrace new challenges. Upon returning to the United States, I wanted a change of scenery. I moved to Phoenix, Arizona, to capitalize on the real estate opportunities.

There was a significant demand for single-family subdivisions. There was a shortage of houses. People were moving to Arizona. People move to Arizona for several reasons, including a lower cost of living, a strong job market, and desirable weather. The state provides a rare combination of natural beauty, economic opportunities, and lifestyle benefits. Although the heat in Arizona can be a concern, the dry climate, and the chance to avoid harsh winters draw many people.

Trouble was evident in a 205-unit townhome subdivision. Looking for real estate opportunities, one could recognize the challenging elements that would reward and challenge an entrepreneur. The completed models required additional upgrades. The company had about five units presold, but the construction process was slow. All the required off-site improvements had not been completed, such as the perimeter fencing around the subdivision, the French drains were not completed other details.

The out-of-state owners from California accepted an offer. Having experience in purchasing properties such as apartments and strip centers with nothing down, this real estate transaction presented another opportunity. The offer included, "Subject to sellers crediting the buyer $125,000.00 toward completing the required improvements." With zero down, the bank approved the financing for 2.5 million dollars. Once the escrow closed, I received a check for $125,000. I now have operating capital.

We upgraded the models by adding skylights to the kitchen and bathrooms. Innovative model home displays were generated, such as floor plans of the available models constructed with Plexiglas walls with lights underneath to highlight the display. The display featured lifestyles. People buy lifestyles. We enlisted a top-notch photographer to feature the models. A national magazine article featured the townhouse models under the title "Major Turnaround of a Subdivision."

My competitors flocked to view the models and asked questions. Many tried to conceal their identities. I told them, "I welcome you to ask questions, and you are welcome to look around, as I have examined your products and taken the best ideas to incorporate into my product." Rarely can one produce an entirely new idea or concept. It is easier, less risky, and cheaper to make incremental improvements. All townhouses quickly sold.

During this time, I needed to learn about finances. The Arizona Republic newspaper advertised an accelerated two-year MBA program, encouraging candidates to apply for acceptance. All candidates were required to have references and letters of recommendation from prominent community members. Upon acceptance, the university revealed the possibility of dual enrollment. The university used the "Harvard" process, where all students stayed together in the same class as they progressed through the subjects. I enrolled in two cohorts, enabling me to graduate with "With Distinction" honors in one year. I graduated while I was building subdivisions. I was the only one to receive this award. My thesis was about the process of converting apartments to condominiums, from the highest- and best use feasibility study to the rehabilitation and marketing process. None of the faculty understood the process. It was a new idea and concept.

This was the first condominium conversion completed in Mesa, Arizona. This was during 18% interest. An advantage of a niche market of having a one-bedroom and two-bedroom condominium at a savings of thousands of dollars for the buyer was a win for the buyer and a win for myself. There was no competition.

Afterwards, I was recommended to schedule an appointment in Las Vegas for a second interview with the developer of Green Valley, a city in the future. It was agreed that the position could be resigned at any time, and I would be flown weekly from Phoenix to Las Vegas to participate in the planning, zoning, and construction process. During this time, a valuable lesson was learned. The first thing the developer did was to have his manager arrange a meeting with the various decision-makers that participated in the construction and rezoning matters. Before the public meetings, the developer made decisions that accelerated the process. We learned the value of networking. We learned the value of having personal relationships. The environment was not a favorable fit. I left.

Las Vegas maintains one of the lowest vacancy rates among major U.S. metros. Las Vegas' hospitality-driven economy has protected it from large-scale office downsizing, unlike other cities. The construction of office buildings commenced. First, we held a meeting with all the decision-makers involved in the approval of the office building's construction plans. We decided on the mitigating factors prior to the public hearings. Only the permitted number of decision-makers could attend the meeting. Open Meeting Act laws play a pivotal role in upholding the principles of transparency, accountability, and public participation in the functioning of local governments. These laws mandate that government agencies and public bodies conduct their meetings and decision-making processes in an open and accessible manner.

In the year 1986, I lost millions. A combination of factors, including high inflation and the Federal Reserve's tight monetary policy to curb it, primarily caused the 1980 recession. To fight rising inflation, the Federal Reserve raised interest rates, leading to a sharp decline in economic activity, a decline in consumer spending, and a 10% annual decline in gross national product.

Las Vegas office/warehouse construction

The recession resulted in a decline in industrial production, a rise in unemployment, and a temporary halt in retail sales and home construction. Despite making giant sums of money, I called in my subcontractors and informed them, "There will be a cash-flow problem in the future." Raised as the son of a preacher, I learned the value of treating others with respect. I was. The contractors feared they would not receive payment. The speed of the funds slowed down. Although all the bills were current, liquidity became a problem. Construction slowed down. We called another meeting to inform everyone that we needed to work together and everything would be OK. Construction slowed even more. From a poor background to having more than I imagined, I was having a gut-wrenching experience.

My back was experiencing spasms. No matter what the doctors did, the stress caused my back muscles to "charlie horse" and caused a misalignment of my lower back. This required back surgery. During my hospitalization, I declared bankruptcy. Gone were my things. No airplane, no corvette, no mansion, nothing. My world was imploding. My wife was sneaking around to see other men. I got a second divorce.

I learned valuable life lessons. I learned failure is a description of an event. Failure can be an obstacle or an opportunity for growth. We get to decide. Time to reassess and rebuild. Time to reevaluate and self-reflect. It's time to apply the lessons we've learned. It's time to look forward to a better and brighter future.

Bakersfield, here I come. I wanted to generate possibilities and opportunities. As I drove into Bakersfield, turning into a restaurant, a friend yelled from his car, "What are you doing? Pull over." In the parking lot, we scheduled an appointment to meet. I had no idea what he wanted. He asked me to be the developer, builder, and arranger of financing for a 300-unit apartment complex in Rosamond, California. He informed me he had to "Get rid of a man" I did not want to be associated with. This man was his financial advisor. His ethics were questionable. We agreed that I would be on a standby basis for 90 days at full salary until he terminated this man.

While waiting for the approvals for financing, I wrote the specifications for the Honda test track facilities for the friend who owned an engineering firm. This was a challenging assignment. How can we replicate a worn and weathered freeway section on a circular test track? We designed different sections of the test track to replicate various specifications of existing roadways. We based the Honda test track specifications on California Caltrans freeway standards and adjusted them for the current road conditions we were replicating.

Imagine, while rebuilding one's personal life and professional life, having lost millions, receiving a letter from the IRS? The letter demanded $350,000 ASAP. The Internal Revenue Service explained in a meeting that I owed the money because I had undergone a voluntary foreclosure of 100 fourplexes, which relieved me of the mortgage obligation. The relief of the money constituted a capital gain. I informed them I had lost millions, and the loss would more than offset the "gain." However, my efforts were in vain. How can one be held liable for a gain when they have lost everything?

This was during a time when short sales were beginning to become normal for real estate owners who owed more money on their property than it was worth. I had noticed a popular real estate broker in Sacramento, California, was advertising short sales, which prompted me to contact the broker and explain the danger of selling short sales. After consulting tax attorneys, the broker agreed to add to his real estate contracts, "If a taxable event occurs from this sale, it is the seller's obligation." We all learn.

I felt strongly that I did not owe the IRS $350,000. It took me five years to reach an agreement with the IRS. I had to pay $5,000 in cash and agree to probation to avoid being in arrears for five years. In the meantime, while negotiating with the IRS, I looked to prove to them I would never be able to pay this unfair obligation. I would be a teacher.

The IRS later changed the law to prevent people from having to pay taxes when they had a mortgage reduced or forgiven.

CHAPTER 10

SECOND BACKPACKING ADVENTURE

Reflecting on my experiences and excitement from backpacking, I felt eager to explore more destinations. I visited Honolulu, Hawaii. I lived there while attending university, so I know the area well. I asked a travel agency, "Where can I go to experience Hawaii 100 years ago?" They replied, "Cook Islands."

I had no idea where the Cook Islands were located. Upon reaching Rarotonga, the Cook Islands' largest and most populous island, my desire was to delve into its exploration.

The island is small. Rarotonga is the center of a quaint paradise that is sure to captivate your attention. Rarotonga, the hub of the Cook Islands, has so much to see and do, yet it remains pristine.

There were no traffic lights, no McDonald's, and no buildings taller than the highest coconut tree. There was a road all around it. A small mountain range ran through the middle.

Most hostels have a day room where people meet and chat. Wanting to explore the island, I asked, "What is the best way to do so?" The consensus was that the best way to cross the island is to go to the brown house, turn right, and follow the trail across the mountain. The trail began as a simple footpath with no markers. It turned into a steep trail.

Rarotonga, Cook Islands

Ropes aided the climb. Eventually, after reaching the top of the mountain, there were no further paths, just a 20-foot flattened area. A large antenna was visible across the canyon. Since it was still morning, I decided to go down the canyon and up to the antenna. I could follow a road down the mountain to the other side of the island.

Dressed in shorts and a T-shirt with a butt pack that held water, and an underwater camera strapped to my waist, I was eager to begin the process. Knowing there were no poisonous or wild animals, I tumbled, fell, and enjoyed the no-trail exploration with the goal of reaching the antenna site. The antenna site was reached at midday. What? No road. The mountain top was a very narrow ridge. The erosion had carved a sharp decline on the mountain.

The jungle consisted of three levels of growth, which made it challenging to avoid falling down the mountain. Every boy scout knows when you are lost; the best way to find your way out is to locate a stream and follow it. What seemed simple became a challenge. I discovered a small waterfall after traveling a considerable distance. Initially, I could jump over small waterfalls. I could get around the bigger waterfalls by walking uphill parallel to the stream.

This was done multiple times. One large waterfall required walking uphill to bypass. I walked across a large mudslide that was moist and slippery, leading to a barren area devoid of any vegetation. By digging down into the mud, I would find a rock or root to hold on to. When the root broke and sent me crashing downhill toward the rocks below in the stream, my worst fear came true. The only thing between the jagged rocks and me was a small 3-inch tree. As I tumbled down, I stretched out my body to stop my fall and grabbed the tree with my left hand. The sudden jolt was massive. At first, I did a "Does everything work?" check. I could hear the rocks that I had dislodged crashing down into the stream below. I noticed that my left eye was seeing only red. I swiped at it to see blood on my left hand, knowing not to let go of the tree with my right hand. My head struck the tree, knocking off the bark. I restored my left eye by wiping off the blood. No one in the world knew where I was.

Challenges. I had always enjoyed a challenge. No one in the world knew where I was. I was alone, stuck about 100 feet above the stream with no way out. I am not one to panic. After careful cost-benefit analysis and observations, my best option was to begin carefully exploring the mud for handholds, anything—rocks, roots, whatever I could find. The mountain was too steep to simply slide down. I had to stairstep zigzag my way down. I learned a valuable life lesson. Please take a moment to slow down, evaluate the situation, consider all available options, and then proceed.

Back to the stream. I washed myself and felt invigorated. I had successfully overcome the challenge. I successfully met the challenge.

What should I do if I hear a large waterfall in the dark? I did not know whether I should jump over it or go around it. The canyon was very steep. Going up one side or the other side was not possible. In the pitch-black dark, another waterfall was heard. Inching my way forward to the edge, sitting on the edge of the waterfall, I listened to the sound of the water hitting below. Was it landing on the rocks or into a pool of water?

I began to reflect on what I did in a similar challenge of jumping. I remember jumping into soft dirt with my neighbor as a teenager from the roof of a house. As we developed courage, we would leap off the house's edge. We put on a blindfold and jumped once we had mastered this. Not being able to see where I would land was like jumping with into this stream. Wow, the sound of the waterfall hitting the stream below sounded like it was hitting a pool of water rather than hitting the rocks. I had no time to dwell on the moment. I must move on and get out of this canyon. Mustering up courage, I jumped, not knowing when to brace for what kind of landing I would experience. Sometimes life is like that. You assess a range of factors, eliminate the riskiest options, and act.

The stream had become larger. I could not see my hand in front of me. The jungle trees crisscrossed the stream, constantly smacking me. The donga trees were the worst. They are a hardwood tree that starts out with a small-diameter, flexible trunk. After falling hundreds of times, I felt a sharp rock inches from my mouth. I knew I would get hurt if I continued. I felt a flat rock in the middle of the stream. I curled on the rock, anxiously looking up at the trees, hoping to see the stars. Should it rain, I would have to cling to the stream's edge. As I lay there exhausted, I suddenly saw a blue flash in the water next to me and in the tree above me. Wow! That is an electric eel. I had been wading in this stream all day with electric eels. Enough! I refused to return to the stream. It was a long night of constantly looking out for animals and the stars. Dawn. What a welcome site. The jungle was denser than I had imagined. It was difficult walking in the daylight.

The trees, grass, and vegetation were dense. Imagine my surprise when I heard a rooster crow! I knew I was back in civilization. After walking more, I came across a dirt road. A flatbed truck came back. It stopped. The driver looked at me in disbelief. I had not considered how I looked. I had blood and mud everywhere. Thankfully, I climbed onto the back of the truck. The people at the hostel were shocked to see this form walk back to his bed. The shower was good!

After two days, the island of Rarotonga was fully explored. There is much more to explore in other areas. I wanted to visit Fiji, an island that is approximately 1,499 miles west of the Cook Islands. Fiji is a bigger and more civilized island that would provide more to discover. Fiji is in the central Pacific Ocean; Fiji's geography has made it both a destination and a crossroads for migrations for many centuries.

Again, a hostel in Nandi was found that unfortunately had bedbugs. Imagine waking up in the middle of the night feeling something moving around in your shorts, biting you. As I shed my shorts, I uncovered a bedbug. It awakens you quickly. After I requested a new room, my situation improved.

Nadi, Fiji, is worth visiting, particularly as a starting point for exploring the rest of the islands. It is a diverse and bustling city, offering a mix of local culture and attractions, and is convenient for accessing nearby beaches and resorts.

Donga Trees, Fiji

CHAPTER 11

FIJI ISLANDS – CONSIST OF OVER 300 ISLANDS.

Fiji shoreline

The ocean was not far away. Walking to the nearest boat harbor, a bulletin board had many papers attached. Out of curiosity, each was read. One was a notice asking for a volunteer to assist in building a raft from bamboo, named Kontinue, the local name for bamboo, BiliBili.

Rob, the author of the notice, was the nephew of the new Prime Minister, Sitiveni Rabuka. Rob wanted to assist the Prime Minister's desire to restore the old customs of Fiji.

Since the early 1900s, individuals from India have been involved in fieldwork in Fiji. Due to their industrious nature and financial practices, they became prominent landowners, taking over significant portions of land initially owned by native Fijians.

Prime Minister Sitiveni Rabuka emerged suddenly from obscurity on 14 May 1987 when he staged a military coup. He walked into Parliament with an AK-47 to take control. It was a bloodless coup. He reasserted ethnic Fijian supremacy. There was a brain drain when Prime Minister Sitiveni Rabuka disenfranchised the Indians, not allowing them to own land. Many of the Indians left Fiji.

Upon contact with Rob, he suggested moving to a village on the Rewa River, the longest and widest river in Fiji. The Rewa originates in Tomanivi, the highest peak in Fiji, and flows southeast for 145 km, or about ninety miles, to Laucala Bay. He knew the chief of the village. I could stay in his hut. There was no electricity. He told me he would arrange for the locals in the highlands to cut bamboo and float it down the river Rewa to the village I would be staying in.

He traded a rugby football to about 30 men from the highland village for an all-day chore of chopping the bamboo down and tying it into bundles to float down the river. The bamboo was giant, more than six inches in diameter and over thirty feet long. The bamboo was on the way. I had to relocate to the village next to the river by the ocean.

Walking down a jungle path on my way to the village, I met two Mormon missionaries wearing clean white shirts. They greeted me by name. I was shocked. How did they know my name? They smiled and asked if I had heard of the "coconut express." They explained it was the way people in the bush communicated.

People would greet each other after saying "Bula. " The most typical question, rather than "How are you?" is "Where are you going?" After the first greeting, news was shared. The village chief was great. He thought I was a wealthy American.

He asked me if I could connect their generator to each hut. After a cursory examination, I decided each hut had the two wires wired together. It was too big a task to explain, so I had to redo what they had done.

When a pig squealed in the morning, one would know there was a pig for dinner. There was no refrigeration. I slept in the chief's wife's bed with a mosquito net.

Men's needs are prioritized over women's and children's. Men's needs come first. For example, my first meal was an entire huge fish with its eyes staring at me. I declined, saying, "I was full." After declining, the chief ate first, then his wife, and then the children.

Rob was enthusiastic about helping others. He had met Mother Teresa and established a trust fund to benefit children with crutches and wheelchairs. He had dual citizenship with Australia and the United States. He had never had a wage-earning job. He always traded things to obtain what he wanted. He got his sailboat using the barter system.

He was always on the move to search for children who needed wheelchairs or crutches. An example of his wanting to help others was when he burned each scabies-infected hut's bed covers to eradicate scabies. Scabies is a significant health issue in Fiji, with a high prevalence reported across various age groups and ethnicities. The scabs are enormous.

They can be found anywhere on the body. Children were the most affected. They had scabs all over their bodies.

The building site was chosen to be near the village but in a protected small bay on the Rewa River. Standing in the water was a daily occurrence while constructing the Kontinue raft. I tied thousands of knots both with vines and nylon string. Stainless steel straps reinforced all the connections.

It took about a month to complete the construction process, working seven days a week. Each day consisted of ten hours of working on the raft. I had no time to socialize with the villagers. Rob was the go-to man. He enjoyed mingling and socializing with the villagers.

Kontinue Raft 50' X 15' looked like this.

The Rewa River, Fiji

The Rewa River is the longest and most significant stream in Fiji. It is in north-central Viti Levu Island on the flanks of Tomanivi, where bamboo grows abundantly. Fiji's highest point, which is 4,344 feet (1,324 meters) tall, flows southeast for ninety miles (145 km) to its mouth at Laucala (Lauthala) Bay on the southeast coast, near Suva, the national capital. In the highlands, along the Rewa river, all the men in the village harvested a large amount of six-inch-diameter bamboo. I had never seen bamboo this large.

The river drains one-third of the island, and its valley and fertile deltas support vegetables, rice, and dairy production. Small steamers can navigate upstream for fifty miles (80 km). It was a perfect location to construct the Kontinue.

Building the bamboo raft was a challenge. Rob's first wish was simply building a raft to incorporate the old ways of using vines to hold the bamboo raft together. Fiji has over 300 islands. His plan was to sail around these islands, displaying how their old construction methods would work. My idea was more audacious. Why not build a huge bamboo raft and sail to the Opera House in Sydney, Australia? Looking at the globe, it was a simple task of sailing six weeks in the Pacific Ocean and making a right-hand turn to the Opera House. The voyage would generate all kinds of publicity.

Wow! What a challenge. I had never sailed. Rob had a sailboat. Rob shared his extensive sailing experiences. I would rely on his ability as the captain of our bamboo raft. He got busy recruiting our sailing crew. Our needs were specific. We needed someone who could navigate and sail using the stars, ocean currents, and wind. We needed another crew member who knew how to fish and what kind of sea creatures were good to eat. We also needed someone with prior sailing experience. We decided to build the Australia-bound bamboo raft! My job was to construct it. Rob was not part of the building process.

The construction process was unique. My research included reading Thor Heyerdahl, who is notable for his Kon-Tiki expedition in 1947, in which he drifted/sailed 8,000 km (5,000 mi) across the Pacific Ocean in a primitive hand-built balsa raft from South America to the Tuamotu Islands, near Tahiti. After his successful experience, he again built another raft from reeds called the Tigris. The goal was to show that trade and migration may have connected Mesopotamia with the Indus Valley civilization in present-day Pakistan and western India.

The Tigris raft was constructed in Al Qurnah, Iraq, and navigated with its international crew through the Persian Gulf to Pakistan, eventually reaching the Red Sea. Coupled with my experience as an engineer and building many types of structures, I felt comfortable accepting the challenge. My prior building process always started with blueprints. From now on, the building process was entirely intuitive. Utilizing my knowledge and experiences, the process began. Initially following the old ways, upon reflection, I augmented the construction process with stainless steel straps borrowed from the road department. Utilizing solely reeds presented a significant challenge. The constant movement of the bamboo bundles and the stress of navigating the unknown waves made me uneasy. The road department used stainless-steel straps to attach signs to telephone poles. They had a clamp to secure the ends. The bamboo poles were long. We trimmed the ends to a consistent length of fifty feet. To manage the inevitable friction in the ocean, we tied the bamboo into five large bundles, with truck tires separating them. This process took over a month of daily effort.

My people skills improved during construction. What a difference in lifestyles. We tried to include local talent in the building process. This attempt was not successful. The work ethic was not there. To those people, I was considered a novelty because I was a wealthy American. Rob would encourage this impression. My hands were sore from tying thousands of nylon string knots and bundling the vines and tying them into knots. I employed three distinct joining methods—stainless-steel bands, vines, and nylon string—to ensure our safety during a six-week sailing expedition in unpredictable ocean conditions. Everything was triple tied. The locals watched me.

Village life was challenging, exciting, and strange. The customs were different. The chief held a position of exaltation and adoration, not one easily accessible.

Using three bamboo sections, separated by truck tires, the Kontinue was 15 feet wide and 30 feet long.

The evenings were unique. Every evening, the men would gather in a separate hut to drink the Fijian beverage known as kava, also referred to as "grog" or "yaqona."

It is traditional to offer a bundle of yagona roots to the chief of a Fijian village when first arriving. If the chief accepts the roots in this sevusevu ceremony, he offers protection and hospitality to the visitor.

Drinking kava, which tastes like earthy water, produces a mild numbness to the lips and mouth and can be quite soporific. These shrubs grow about two meters tall and are often seen along roads and near homes in the Fijian countryside.

Overall, the village people were friendly and open to suggestions. An interesting fact I learned is that the light-skinned villagers were admired and treated better than others.

Preparing Kava

It's a mildly narcotic and sedative beverage made from the root of the Piper methysticum plant. Kava is used in ceremonies for its calming and numbing effects. The practice of consuming kava is embedded in social events and workplace environments. People use it similarly to how we would use coffee. The chief had his own polished coconut half shell to drink from. The rest of us shared a hollowed half coconut shell to drink the kava. After each drink, each person would say, "mudda." A non-church guitar accompanied communal singing. After drinking kava, some would fall asleep. Once most of the villagers had fallen asleep, the singing and guitar playing slowed down and eventually ended the drinking session.

The village people were friendly. The custom in the village was when a person wanted something, they simply took it. The chief "borrowed" a tub from one of the villagers. They complained to me. I said, "This was the tradition, and they knew it." They resolved the issue according to their customs. Countless villagers would watch me eat dinner in the evenings. I was a novelty.

The raft required a sail. Many discussions focused on the best sail for a raft with daggerboards. Rob said he would get one. We discussed ways to hang the sail. We decided I would construct a four-legged mast that resembled an oil derrick. The mast was secured to the raft by attaching it to both sides. Since I had worked in the oilfield on derricks, I was familiar with the basic design. We decided a 30-foot-tall derrick would work for the sail requirements. Our rigging played a pivotal role in the safe and efficient handling of heavy loads. Our rigging was a simple combination of ropes connected to the mast and to the sail. Our sail was a single-mast junk rig. It could sail upwind at 3 degrees! My research had indicated that daggerboards were needed for our raft.

The purpose of the daggerboard (or any keel) is to balance the force of the wind on the sails. A sailboat needs a daggerboard or keel to sail upwind; otherwise, it would drift sideways. During a storm, daggerboards can help reduce the tendency of a small boat to tip over ("breach") due to waves. A 4' x 8' piece of plywood was cut to 2' x 6' to mimic a daggerboard. It worked outstandingly, enabling the raft to sail upwind.

CHAPTER 12

SAILING FROM FIJI TO AUSTRALIA ON RAFT

Most villagers gathered at our construction site to celebrate the launch of our raft. We pushed off into the Rewa River to sail into the ocean. Our crew was excited. Multiple deportations of Fijians from Australia occurred due to inadequate documentation and strict immigration policies. The Fiji natives viewed Australia as an opportunity to make money and enjoy a more prosperous life. It was a celebration of odd people doing strange things!

The tide had gone out. The river was flowing faster than normal. Floating down the river, we noticed a frenzy of shark feeding near the mangroves. The sharks were eating the fish that were feeding on the mangroves. We avoided the sharks. Rounding a river bend, I could see a huge donga tree overhanging the river on the outside of the bend. I told Rob, "Watch for that tree." The Kontinue raft mast hit the overhanging Donga tree. The 50-foot-long, 15-foot-wide raft groaned as it struggled against the tree.

Slowly, the raft, which we called the "Kontinue," began to tilt toward the river. We quickly tied the raft to the tree. The raft settled in a 90-degree tilt from the river. Slowly, the 30-foot-tall mast, which had no sail, began to collapse as two of its supporting legs snapped. The mast fell from the edge of the raft to the top of the river. It did not hit our shack/crew quarters. As the mast collapsed, the raft settled back into the swirling river around us. My priority was to repair our mast and erect it again. While I instructed a crewmember to crawl out on the mast and cut the vines holding the bamboo poles in place, he swung his machete, missed, and slipped, disappearing into the river. The concern about the sharks created a fear we had lost a crew member.

He surfaced next to the raft and crawled onto the deck without a word. He was worried about losing his machete. The villagers loved their machetes. They kept losing theirs and asking me to buy them another. He had a gash across and down his abdomen about an inch wide. I could see his muscles. They were gray. He was barely bleeding. Ignoring him, all hands were busy repairing the damage and erecting the mast. Having erected the mast and tied it off at the tree, attention was given to securing the mast to the deck again.

While absorbed in the task of securing the mast, the injured crew member untied it from the tree. I had no idea why. The mast fell and struck me on the top of my head. The impact was akin to an explosion, causing me to collapse onto my knees. I could not breathe. Rob began cursing the crewmember. As soon as I could talk, I asked Rob to ignore the crewmember and let us get this raft going. The rest of the day, I felt weird. I had no energy. My thinking was in simple sentences. While in the Bay Area, we hoisted our sail. We learned to coordinate the daggerboards with the setting of the single sail. Our sail was triangle shaped. Rob had traded things for our "free sail." He was adept at bartering. He had convinced Sony Corporation to donate camera equipment to enable us to document our demonstration of Fijian skills in sailing the ocean using the old ways. We had stockpiled coconuts on the deck. We did not lose any coconuts. The coconuts were a major part of our food source. We would augment it with fish we caught during the trip.

It was a strange feeling to see the shoreline disappear. Reality began to settle throughout my body. We were really going to sail in the ocean. With resolve, I shrugged off the apprehension. We learned how to sail the raft into the wind, coordinating with the daggerboards. It was a thrill! Relying on others to determine direction and sailing method was spooky.

I was not in control. I learned the basics of the sun and stars' orientation and how to keep a constant direction. Obtaining rest was difficult. The raft was in constant motion. Everything was wet. I relied on Rob's experience in managing the sailing process and on a crewmember who claimed to know how to navigate using the stars. He said he had done it many times, sailing from one island to another in Fiji. Spooky. We had no radios. People at the Yacht Club said, "You stupid-ass bastards will not make it, and you will expect us to save your ass." This challenge was real.

Experiencing the aquarium of sea life, which swam between the truck tires separating the bamboo bundles, was wonderful. What various creatures. Most of the organisms were not identified. Rob woke me up a few nights later, his voice filled with panic. He screamed, "What do I do?" He was the expert; I had no idea about what he was talking about. We were crashing into a reef somewhere out in the ocean.

My first concern was to ensure the raft was seaworthy and would not be damaged. I ordered the crew members to gather bamboo and cut it to a length that would shield the raft from any damage until we could figure out how to sail away from this reef. By inserting and securing vertical lengths of bamboo that would hit the reefs and protect our raft from any damage, we managed to move away from the reefs.

I had lost my confidence in Rob. It was time to return to Fiji. Time was lost wandering around until daylight. The sun, to me, was a much better direction finder. Soon, the sight of birds and wave patterns became a reassuring indication of our familiarity with the Fiji seas, which helped us determine our location and direction. in our cancellation of our ill-fated exercise to show the old ways of sailing. I had all the challenges I needed. I learned the power of resilience. I learned that being goal-oriented isn't enough; one must also be adaptable and resilient.

I was ready to return to California. The IRS never went away. They contacted me asking when I could pay $500,000. Sometimes in life, if you cannot beat them, it may be better to join them. The IRS possessed copies of newspapers and magazines that contained articles discussing my success. At this point, five years had passed while negotiating and meetings, and I received my first notice from the IRS. They offered a settlement. I became an educator to demonstrate that I would never be able to pay off my $500,000 debt, as educators do not earn enough money. Being an educator changed and enhanced my life. To me, business was warfare. Take no prisoners. An educator experiences empathy, nurturing, and caring. While teaching science, I would explain an idea or concept, and the "aha" moment would show in their eyes. I would get tears in my eyes. I was shocked and embarrassed. I would have to walk away.

Getting qualified to teach was a frustrating and challenging experience. After contacting the personnel department, they informed me they needed science and math teachers. I told them, "I like science." They replied,

"Well, you must have a teaching credential with a science endorsement." There were no shortcuts. This was the bureaucratic education system with which I was dealing. I earned the teacher's credential through arduous coursework. I obtained another master's degree in curriculum.

Let us discuss science credentials now. Contacting the personnel department again, after more prodding and questioning, they informed me that a science credential could be awarded if one passed the National Teachers Examination (NTE). The "national teaching exam" refers to various standardized tests used to assess prospective teachers' knowledge and skills needed for obtaining state teaching licenses. These exams can vary by state and subject area but commonly assess general knowledge, subject matter ability, and pedagogical knowledge.

In addition, they said, "It is difficult to obtain; only the top 25 percentile are awarded the credential." I had forgotten what the difference was between a percentile and a percentage. I learned a percentage is a part of a whole, expressed as a fraction of one hundred. For example, if you get 80 out of 100 questions right on a test, your percentage score is 80%. A percentile, on the other hand, shows your position relative to others in a group or population. For example, if you score in the 90th percentile on a test, it means you performed better than 90% of the other students who took the same test. Outstanding! I said, "Sign me up." I purchased Graduate Record Exam (GRE) science exam books and four other science related exam books to learn the science vocabulary and studied these for one week. I was ready. I received my science credential. In addition, the multiple subjects, and administrative credentials were awarded via testing. Not only could I teach science, but I was also qualified to be a principal, or Superintendent. In addition, I completed a PhD program in organization management.

After ten years as an educator, progressing from a science teacher to Assistant Principal, to Principal; having reinvented myself caring for others, I was looking for a change of pace.

My desire for a change of pace was motivated by a School Board that agreed with a student and her parents to reinstate her in school after I had completed all the mitigating steps of counselor meetings, a staff psychologist meeting and a Student Attendance Review Board (SARB).
This is a group that helps resolve student attendance and behavior issues. SARBs, often composed of representatives from various youth-serving agencies, work with students and families to find solutions using available school and community resources. They aim to divert students from the juvenile justice system and address the root causes of attendance problems. The School Board changed my mind, and I had to reinstate her back into high school. Within a week she was cutting classes again. I had lost control of my school. I was being micro-managed. In the meantime, flipping houses provide the cash needed to pay the bills.

CHAPTER 13

MOVED TO STOCKTON, RETIRED

I retired again to Pismo Beach, California. I learned to dance and enjoyed meeting new people. Dancing at the Madonna Inn with a live big band was a highlight. A recent challenging experience was persuading my 86-year-old mother to motor up in my 30-foot cabin cruiser to Stockton, California, from Morrow Bay, California. It took four days. What an adventure! After spending six months updating, sanding, polishing for days, and installing new equipment, the "Glenda Fae" was ready to sail on an adventure. With no ocean-going experience and learning how to operate the instruments with no shore in sight, the boat performed flawlessly. Initially, the swells were coming from the north. This meant sailing "upwind."

There were no other boats or ships visible. The twelve-foot swells made the boat come out of the water. One had to slow down to stop the pounding. My brave mother quietly went below to the dining table with a black plastic bag between her legs to view her lunch. She never complained. Initially we sailed from Avila Beach, California. Morro Bay is only about 45 miles from Avila Beach. It took us six hours and 60 gallons of fuel because of the rough weather. The first thing my mother wanted to do after refilling the fuel tanks was to sing karaoke. It was the best singing she had done. We both possessed a passion for life.

Throughout these experiences, we embraced the philosophy of action over words. The learning process of being an entrepreneur is not about reckless risk-taking but thorough research and mitigating uncertainties. By carefully balancing risk and reward, I established parameters that paved the way for success.

I understood that true success is not measured by wealth but by self-acceptance and the ability to look in the mirror with pride. Failures became steppingstones, each offering invaluable lessons and guiding me toward personal growth. Learning to fail your way to success is OK.

I learned success has many meanings; a joyful family is priority number one. Having money gives one more choice. It is not a measure of success. As my finances improved, I learned the "idea" and "notion" of success are both related to the concept of achievement, but "idea" suggests a concrete, specific goal, while "notion" is a more general, vague, and often personal feeling of what success entails.

Success, at its core, is about achieving what one desires, whether it's a specific goal or a broader sense of accomplishment.

The 36' Glenda Fae below deck had restroom, shower, kitchen and queen size bed. I sailed from Avila Beach to Stockton, California ocean cruise. New navigation, instruments.

In retirement, I began to reflect on what I did in the USAF. Many of the activities I did were illegal. It was all shrouded in being a top-secret activity. My concern is how to manage these individuals and ensure they understand accountability. Everyone needs to be accountable. For example, when I owned a Honda dealership, the parts department had only one cash drawer. I was always short. When each person had their own cash drawer, I was never short.

Resolving my angsts, I authored a book, "Eyes Wide Shut: An Enigma." It is available on Amazon. This process took two years. The subject matter required that it be presented as a fictional account to prevent me from going to prison. The subject matter was based on my activities with everything changed. My concern about the subject matter prevented me from marketing this book. It is sold by word of mouth.

My service-connected employment created a unique environment. We had weekly security examinations that reinforced security policies and protocols. We were constantly informed the "bad guys" would try to obtain information from you. A slip of the lip would sink a ship philosophy was used. Having a spy around me in prior years that no one knew was a spy for the "bad guys" made it real.

This heightened my concern about being on the alert. An example of this is Edward Snowden, who worked at the same facility as I did, but later. Edward Joseph Snowden was a former American NSA intelligence contractor and whistleblower who leaked classified documents revealing the existence of global surveillance programs.

In 2013, while working as a government contractor, Snowden leaked highly classified information from the National Security Agency (NSA). He was indicted for espionage.

His disclosures revealed multiple global surveillance programs, most run by the NSA and the Five Eyes intelligence alliance with the cooperation of telecommunication companies and European governments and prompted a cultural discussion about national security and individual privacy.

It is worth noting that the government has been dishonest. The agencies before Congress said they would stop surveilling the public's phone conversations. The agencies simply hired other companies to conduct the same surveillance.

This environment prompted me to assess what I did in the USAF. One of my most difficult challenges was to integrate what I did and who was accountable. The top Secrete activities requires everyone to "compartmentalize." This is to minimize the damage to US security in the event on spies for another country or is captured. Questions such as, "How does one manage people with Top Secrete Security Clearances?" The "need to know" philosophy is paramount. No one could ask questions about what you did.

During this time frame, I had a need to write about what I did. Given that most of what I did was classified, I decided to write a fiction book based upon my activities.

It is a huge challenge to stare at a blank computer screen and contemplate what to write. This was the beginning of my writing career. I presently have 20 books published on Amazon's Kindle. The process is a learning process. I have a lot to learn. I have chosen to write books in many different genres, including a biography about my mother, Glenda Fae Rucks and an autobiography about me. I hope you enjoy the process as much as I have created the books.

CHAPTER 14

TRANSFORMATION AND TRIUMPH

Less is more. After authoring the book, "Eyes Wide Shut: An Enigma," available on Amazon at https://www.amazon.com/Eyes-Wide-Dallas-Wayne-Thompson/dp/0984685006 I was creating a Facebook platform to help people learn about the book. One of my Facebook friends, whom Facebook had suggested, was someone I dated 42 years ago. It was my future wife, Connie J. Thompson!

After dating me for a brief time, she dumped me. Years later, I found out why. She thought, "I was too good to be true." I was a real estate developer and had an airplane, a new Corvette, and the lifestyle of a millionaire. This time, we dated a year and were married. Her 39-year marriage had ended

Despite Arizona being known as a "dry heat area," there is skiing!

when he died. She waited two years after his death before she started dating again. It is remarkable what a man will do when he is in love! I moved back to Bakersfield, California. I married my best friend. As of this book's writing, we have been married for almost 14 years.

John Steinbeck immortalized Weedpatch, where my mother arrived at the age of seven, in his 1939 novel "Grapes of Wrath." Like many other Dust Bowlers, who have revived the once-derogatory word "Okie" as a term of endearment and source of pride, she can vividly summon the chapters of her life: of no food, no money, and desperate for shelter on hot summer nights cooled only by bedsheets soaked with a hose and then draped over the tent. My mother had been a lively person who I enjoyed being around. Her roots were depression refugees from the Dust Bowl era. She met my father at Weedpatch, California. Steinbeck and his photographer, Dorothy Lange, saw my relatives and took pictures of them. The children were playing in the mud. My relatives believed they were the targets of mockery. They grabbed the camera, threw it into the mud, and stomped on it to ruin the pictures.

My mother passed when she was 90 years old. The event was an awakening to me. This meant I was next in line to die. I convinced my wife to retire. She was working in Child Protective Services, Bakersfield, California.
We viewed Lakeside, Arizona, as a place to retire. Lakeside is a town in Navajo County, Arizona, United States. According to the 2020 census, the population of the town is 4,557. Lakeside is a popular summer resort and second-home area for Arizona desert residents. Having recently retired, we eagerly set out to explore the area together. Lakeside, Arizona, offers various outdoor activities and attractions, particularly in and around the White Mountains. With an elevation of 7,000 feet, the area boasts diverse landscapes, including the Apache/Sitgreaves National Forest.

As a resort area, there are over fifty lakes in the Lakeside area, including over 1,000 miles of shoreline along the streams.

The area is called the White Mountains region. Additionally, there are dozens of streams and small rivers, making it a popular destination for water sports and recreation. Popular activities include hiking, biking, horseback riding, fishing, and exploring the White Mountains Trail System.

Tourists mostly visit during the hot summers. The temperature here in the summer is around 75 degrees. At the same time, in Phoenix, Arizona, it is 115 degrees.

My wife soon wanted a more active life. She started working for the state of Arizona's Child Protective Services.

Being alone and wanting to be active, I applied to the Apache tribe to teach science. As an optimist, my goal was to help the Apache students achieve grade status in all their studies. The existing grade level for the students was 98%, below their grade level. What a challenge! I wanted to make a positive difference.

The Fort Apache Historic District is the original site of the Fort Apache military post. Fort Apache was a major outpost during the Apache Wars (1871-1886) and stayed a military post until 1922. In 1923, the fort became the site of the Theodore Roosevelt Indian Boarding School.

Fort Apache illustrates the U.S. government's evolving approaches to the so-called "Indian problem" from the end of the Civil War to the conclusion of World War II. Fort Apache, once a combat post to fight the Indians, underwent a transformation into an educational facility with the aim of assimilating the Indians into mainstream American culture.

Today the White Mountain Apache Tribe and the Fort Apache Heritage Foundation are preserving and interpreting the landmark for a new kind of active duty, as a place to reflect on the past, to maintain Apache cultural traditions, to boost the tribe's sovereignty, and to create opportunities for the tribe's citizens.

Fort Apache School enriched my heritage. My father's mother was a full-blooded Indian. She was half a Cherokee and half Choctaw. She was ashamed of her heritage. During that time, being an Indian was looked down upon.

An example is "Indians cannot drink firewater." I was keen to learn what being a Native American meant. I was keen to learn about their culture and beliefs. I was keen to learn why my grandmother was ashamed to be an Indian. She never obtained her Native American tribe number.

Fort Apache consists of many buildings. Theodore Roosevelt Middle School.

I quickly discovered that the Apache people's culture differed from my own. The statement, "It takes a village to raise a child, is true." Sadly, I must admit my efforts were not successful. After two years, retirement beckoned me again.

I live in a resort area, and the temptation was too great. I had a considerable influence on one student's life. He was smart but was failing. He would not make any effort to pass. At the end of the year, he earned a "C." I was successful in enabling him to care and try. Later, I would meet former students in the store and ask them to share how I had helped them and made a positive difference in their lives. One had graduated with top honors in college!

We decided we would enjoy exploring the United States in a recreational vehicle. Before we could buy one, my wife was diagnosed with stage four cancer. Wow! At the hospital we discussed buying the RV. We decided to fully enjoy every aspect of it. To cheer her on, I bought an RV and a miniature poodle, Tinker Bell. Now, she has a Shih Tzu, Precious, and a poodle. Following additional medical procedures, doctors declared her cancer-free! Amazing!

To achieve cancer-free status, an individual must endure five years without the disease. She now has one more year to go. She has no symptoms. Every 90 days she has blood tests that check for cancer markers. There have been no traces of cancer.

CHAPTER 15

AFTER FOUR RETIREMENTS-BOTH

Retired!

Today, our lives are simple. My wife, Connie, manages our Airbnb and enjoys the fun of meeting people from everywhere.

Our Air B N B – My wife's hobby!

I am 80 years young, and my wife is 70 years young. We are living the best part of our lives. The last 13 years of marriage have been outstanding.

I have been actively living my life instead of merely wishing I had done things differently. It is a challenge not to be taken lightly. My challenges are now my health. Getting old is not for weak or passive people. I may have brain cancer or a meningioma. There are no symptoms. We need to conduct more assessments. My goal of living life to its fullest is achieved every day! There is more. My goal is to discover all that I can and share experiences with my wife.

I have learned life is a process. Process goals focus not on results but on the steps, you take to get them. Process goals are great because you control them; they focus on what you can do to reach a goal, not an uncertain outcome.

Process goals (how you achieve something) must be secondary to performance or learning goals (what you achieve). Success through failure has been a learned process. My life has achieved more than I had dreamed about. Hand in hand, my wife and I eagerly look forward to exploring each day and to learning what new possibilities await us.

My new career as an author has provided a huge learning opportunity and enjoying the creativity of the book writing process. I have learned a lot and have much more to learn. It is an exciting journey. As I have stated, "Process goals focus not on results but on the steps, you take to get them." I enjoy experiencing something new. The process of writing creates an anticipation of excitement! I enjoy the process!

Dallas W. Thompson and Connie J. Thompson

Dallas W Thompson, MBA – With Distinction, MA, PhD OM, Teacher Credential, Multiple and Single Subject; Science, Administrative Credential, Engineering License 344256, General Contractor, FCC First Class License.

Born in Bakersfield, California to "Grapes of Wrath" descendants. Firstborn son of three siblings of a preacher father and piano-playing mother. Raised in a small rural area, having learned to hand-pick cotton and potatoes, he worked for lunch money and a used bicycle in high school. Two sons, Dallas Steven Thompson and Shawn Wayne Thompson, deceased.

EPILOGUE

As I write these final words, the morning sun is streaming through the windows of our home in Lakeside, Arizona, casting long shadows across the desk where I have spent countless hours over the past months, revisiting the journey that has brought me to this moment. At eighty years young, with my beloved wife Connie preparing breakfast in the kitchen and our dogs Precious and Tinker Bell keeping me company, I find myself filled not with a sense of ending, but with anticipation for whatever adventures still await us.

The process of writing this memoir has been both challenging and revelatory. Revisiting the various chapters of my life—from the dust-covered fields of Weedpatch to the boardrooms of successful businesses, from the treacherous waters of the Pacific to the classrooms where I taught Apache children—has reminded me of the extraordinary nature of what might seem like an ordinary American life. More importantly, it has reinforced my belief that every life contains the potential for adventure, growth, and meaningful contribution, regardless of its starting point or the obstacles it encounters.

Looking back over eight decades, I am struck by the realization that the most significant moments in my journey were often the ones that seemed most challenging at the time. The poverty of my childhood, rather than limiting my possibilities, taught me the value of hard work and the importance of seizing opportunities when they arise. The business failures that cost me millions in the 1980s, rather than ending my story, opened new chapters that proved more fulfilling than anything I had previously experienced. The transition from entrepreneur to educator, which initially felt like a step backward, ultimately provided some of the most meaningful work of my life.

These experiences have taught me that resilience is not simply about bouncing back from adversity but about using setbacks as springboards for growth and transformation. The ability to reinvent oneself, to find new sources of meaning and purpose when old ones are exhausted or taken away, may be the most valuable skill anyone can develop in our rapidly changing world.

The reunion with Connie after forty-two years apart was perhaps the greatest gift of my later years. Our marriage has reminded me that love, like adventure, is not limited by age or circumstance. The challenges we have faced together—including her battle with cancer and my own health concerns—have only strengthened our bond and deepened our appreciation for each day we have together. Our current life, managing our Airbnb business and planning new travels, demonstrates that retirement need not mean withdrawal from engagement with the world, but can instead represent a new form of contribution and exploration.

The health challenges that come with aging—the possibility of brain cancer that hangs over my current situation—serve as daily reminders of life's fragility and preciousness. Rather than causing despair, these realities have sharpened my focus on what truly matters: relationships, experiences, and the legacy we leave through our impact on others. The knowledge that my time may be limited has paradoxically freed me to live more fully in the present moment.

One of the most important lessons I hope readers will take from this memoir is that success is not a destination but a process, not a single achievement but a series of adaptations to changing circumstances. The financial success that seemed so important in my thirties and forties gave way to different priorities in my fifties and sixties and continued to evolve today. True success, I have come to believe, is measured not in dollars or achievements, but in our ability to look in the mirror and love the person looking back, despite our imperfections.

This understanding has profound implications for how we approach our careers, our relationships, and our personal development. Rather than pursuing external validation or comparing ourselves to others, we can focus on becoming the best versions of ourselves, on contributing meaningfully to the lives of others, and on leaving the world a little better than we found it.

The adventures that have punctuated my life—from building bamboo rafts in Fiji to teaching in remote schools—have taught me that the most valuable experiences often lie outside our comfort zones. The willingness to embrace uncertainty, to take calculated risks, and to remain curious about the world and its possibilities has been a constant source of energy and renewal throughout my journey. I encourage readers to seek their own adventures, whether they involve travel to distant lands or simply exploring new aspects of their own communities and capabilities.

The business ventures that defined much of my middle years provided their own education in human nature, market dynamics, and the importance of adaptability. The Honda dealership that made me wealthy taught me about the power of relationships and customer service. The real estate developments that followed demonstrated the importance of understanding market cycles and managing risk. The failures that cost me everything reinforced the lesson that external circumstances can change rapidly, but internal resources—knowledge, skills, relationships, and character—remain portable and valuable.

My transition to education in my later career provided a different kind of fulfillment than business success ever had. Working with Apache children at Fort Apache, discovering my own Native American heritage, and witnessing the "aha" moments when students grasped difficult concepts reminded me that the most meaningful achievements often involve helping others realize their potential. This experience reinforced my belief that every stage of life offers opportunities for growth and contribution, and that our most important work may come in chapters we never anticipated. The writing of this memoir has also been an education in the power of storytelling to connect us across differences of background, generation, and circumstance. While my specific experiences may be unique, the emotions and challenges represent the fear of failure, the joy of achievement, the pain of loss, the excitement of discovery—are universal. My hope is that readers will see their own struggles and aspirations reflected in these pages and will find encouragement for their own journeys.

For younger readers, I want to emphasize that the fundamental principles that have guided my life—hard work, resilience, adaptability, and the courage to pursue one's dreams—remain as relevant as ever. The specific opportunities I encountered may not be available to future generations, but the mindset and approach that enabled me to capitalize on them are timeless. The key is to remain alert to possibilities, to develop skills that can be applied across different contexts, and to maintain the flexibility to adapt when circumstances change.

For readers facing their own challenges and setbacks, I want to offer the assurance that failure is indeed "a description of an event" rather than a judgment on personal worth. Every setback contains lessons that can inform future decisions, and every ending creates space for new beginnings. The ability to learn from mistakes, to maintain perspective during difficult times, and to keep moving forward despite uncertainty is perhaps the most valuable skill anyone can develop.

For those in their later years, I want to challenge the conventional narratives about aging and retirement. Connie and I have found our eighties to be among the most fulfilling years of our lives, filled with new experiences, deepening relationships, and continued opportunities for growth and contribution. Age brings its own challenges, but it also brings wisdom, perspective, and often freedom from the pressures and expectations that constrain younger people.

The Airbnb business that Connie manages has become more than just a source of income; it has become a way of connecting with people from around the world, of sharing our home and our stories, and of remaining engaged with the broader human community. The guests who stay with us bring their own stories and perspectives, enriching our lives and reminding us that adventure and discovery can happen in our own backyard as well as in distant lands.

Our plans for continued travel and exploration demonstrate that curiosity and wanderlust need not diminish with age. The RV that sits in our driveway represents not just a vehicle for transportation, but a symbol of our continued commitment to new experiences and discoveries. Whether we are exploring national parks, visiting family and friends, or simply discovering new corners of our own country, we approach each journey with the same sense of anticipation and wonder that has characterized our entire relationship.

The health challenges that we face—my potential brain cancer, the ongoing monitoring of Connie's cancer markers—serve as reminders of life's uncertainty and preciousness. Rather than allowing these concerns to limit our activities or dampen our spirits, we have chosen to use them as motivation to make the most of whatever time we have together. Every day becomes a gift to be unwrapped and appreciated, every experience an opportunity to create lasting memories.

Looking forward to the future, I am filled with gratitude for the journey that has brought me to this point and excitement about the adventures that still await. The memoir you have just read represents not an ending but a milestone, a pause to reflect on the path traveled before continuing forward. There are still places to explore, people to meet, and contributions to make. The story continues.

To the readers who have accompanied me on this journey through the pages of this memoir, I offer my deepest thanks. Your willingness to share my experiences, to consider my perspectives, and to reflect on your own journeys has made the effort of writing this book worthwhile. I hope that you have found in these pages not just entertainment, but inspiration and practical wisdom that you can apply to your own lives.

Remember that every day offers new possibilities, every challenge contains the seeds of growth, and every ending is also a beginning. The dust may have settled on the fields of Weedpatch where my journey began, but the dreams and determination that sustained my parents and their neighbors continue to inspire new generations of Americans seeking to build better lives for themselves and their children.

The American Dream, in all its complexity and contradiction, remains alive and available to those willing to pursue it with courage, persistence, and an open heart. The specific forms it takes may change with each generation, but it's essential promise—that we can transcend our circumstances through effort and determination—endures.

As I close this memoir and return to the daily adventures of life with Connie, I carry with me the lessons learned across eight decades of living: that resilience is more valuable than wealth, that relationships matter more than achievements, that curiosity is the antidote to aging, and that love, in all its forms, is the greatest adventure of all.

The journey continues, and I am grateful to be traveling with my best friend by my side, our faithful dogs at our feet, and the endless possibilities of tomorrow stretching out before us like an open road leading toward the horizon.

To those who are just beginning their own journeys, to those who are in the middle of great challenges or great successes, and to those who are contemplating new chapters in their later years, I offer this simple advice: embrace the adventure, learn from every experience, and never stop believing in the possibility of transformation. The odds may seem overwhelming at times, but as my life has demonstrated, with enough determination and a willingness to keep beginning again, anything is possible.

Against all odds, the journey continues.

Perhaps if a list an example of my learning experiences. I wrote a book about consciousness. Defining consciousness is a huge challenge.

The book format closely follows a PhD Dissertation process. A huge amount of research is required. APA citations are used to inform the reader where I obtain the information. This book is not about my feelings of ideas. It is researched based, and I follow my inquiring mind to determine what consciousness is and its implications. A glossary is included at the end of each chapter to enable the reader to understand the ideas and concepts as I explore the unknown.

The beginning of the process includes an outline of my book. The outline serves as a beacon, a format of knowing what goals must be met to achieve my goal of understanding more about consciousness.

THE PROCESS OF WRITING A BOOK

Develop an Outline

The Universal Mind: Consciousness as the Fundamental Fabric of Reality
A Comprehensive Book Outline for Academic Leaders
Author: Dallas W. Thompson, PhD

Book Overview

This groundbreaking work presents consciousness not as an emergent property of complex biological systems, but as the fundamental, universal, and timeless substrate of all reality. Drawing from rigorous scientific research, mathematical formalism, and philosophical analysis, this book offers a revolutionary paradigm that resolves the "hard problem of consciousness" while providing practical applications for medicine, ethics, technology, and human understanding.

The book synthesizes Integrated Information Theory, panpsychism, cosmic consciousness, and quantum mechanics into a unified framework that demonstrates consciousness as basic to the universe as mass, energy, or space-time. This synthesis provides academic leaders with both theoretical depth and practical applications, positioning consciousness studies as a central discipline for understanding reality itself.

Target Audience and Academic Impact
This work addresses worldwide academic leaders across multiple disciplines: neuroscientists seeking to understand the neural basis of consciousness, philosophers grappling with the mind-body problem, physicists exploring the role of consciousness in quantum mechanics, psychologists investigating altered states and therapeutic applications, and ethicists developing frameworks for global cooperation and environmental stewardship.

The book's interdisciplinary approach ensures relevance across academic boundaries while maintaining the rigor expected in each field. By providing testable hypotheses, mathematical formulations, and empirical predictions, it establishes consciousness studies as a mature scientific discipline capable of generating meaningful research programs and practical applications.

PART I: FOUNDATIONS OF CONSCIOUSNESS STUDIES
Chapter 1: The Great Mystery - Consciousness in Historical Perspective
Pages 1-25
This opening chapter establishes the historical foundation for understanding consciousness as humanity's greatest scientific and philosophical challenge. The chapter traces the evolution of consciousness studies from ancient philosophical inquiries through modern neuroscientific investigations, demonstrating how each era's understanding reflects its dominant worldview while pointing toward universal principles that transcend cultural and temporal boundaries.

The chapter begins with ancient philosophical foundations, examining how early thinkers like Thales, Plato, and Aristotle first grappled with the relationship between mind and matter [1]. Thales' assertion that "everything is full of gods" represents an early panpsychist insight, while Plato's theory of Forms suggests consciousness as fundamental to reality's structure [2]. The chapter explores how Eastern philosophical traditions, particularly Buddhism and Vedanta, developed sophisticated analyses of consciousness that anticipated many contemporary insights about the nature of awareness and its relationship to reality [3].

Medieval and Renaissance developments receive detailed attention, particularly how Islamic philosophers like Al-Ghazali and Averroes preserved and extended Greek philosophical insights while Christian thinkers like Thomas Aquinas attempted to reconcile Aristotelian philosophy with religious doctrine [4]. The Renaissance revival of Platonic ideas through figures like Marsilio Ficino and Pico della Mirandola set the stage for modern consciousness studies by reintroducing concepts of cosmic consciousness and universal mind [5].

The emergence of modern philosophy through René Descartes' dualistic framework receives critical analysis, showing how Cartesian dualism both advanced and constrained consciousness studies [6]. The chapter examines how John Locke's empiricism and Immanuel Kant's critical philosophy attempted to resolve the mind-body problem while inadvertently deepening the explanatory gap between subjective experience and objective reality [7]. Special attention is given to how these philosophical developments influenced the emergence of scientific psychology and neuroscience.

The twentieth century scientific revolution in consciousness studies forms the chapter's climax, examining how behaviorism's rejection of consciousness as unscientific was eventually overcome by cognitive psychology's information-processing approach [8]. The chapter analyzes how neuroscientific discoveries about brain function gradually restored consciousness as a legitimate scientific topic while revealing the profound challenges involved in explaining subjective experience in purely physical terms [9].

The chapter concludes by examining the contemporary renaissance in consciousness studies, triggered by David Chalmers' formulation of the "hard problem" and the development of new theoretical frameworks like Integrated Information Theory [10]. This historical survey demonstrates that while approaches to consciousness have varied dramatically across cultures and centuries, certain core insights about consciousness as fundamental to reality have persisted, suggesting universal principles that transcend particular theoretical frameworks.

Throughout the chapter, extensive quotations from primary sources illustrate how great thinkers across history have struggled with consciousness, providing readers with direct access to the intellectual tradition they are joining. The chapter establishes that contemporary consciousness studies represent not a break from historical inquiry but its culmination, as modern scientific methods finally provide tools adequate to address questions that have fascinated humanity since the beginning of reflective thought.

Chapter 2: The Current Landscape - Major Theories and Their Limitations
Pages 26-50
This chapter provides a comprehensive analysis of contemporary consciousness theories, examining their strengths, limitations, and contributions to understanding while setting the stage for the universal consciousness paradigm. The analysis demonstrates how current theories, despite significant insights, remain incomplete due to their failure to

address consciousness as fundamental rather than emergent.

Global Workspace Theory, developed by Bernard Baars and refined by Stanislas Dehaene, receives detailed examination as the most influential contemporary framework [11]. The chapter explains how GWT proposes consciousness as arising from global broadcasting of information across brain networks, making previously unconscious processing available to multiple cognitive systems simultaneously [12]. While acknowledging GWT's success in explaining access consciousness and its neural correlates, the chapter identifies critical limitations: the theory explains how information becomes globally available but not why this availability should be accompanied by subjective experience [13]. The "broadcast" metaphor, while computationally useful, fails to address why there should be anyone "listening" to the broadcast or why the listening should involve qualitative, subjective experience rather than mere information processing. Integrated Information Theory, developed by Giulio Tononi, receives extensive analysis as the most mathematically rigorous contemporary approach [14]. The chapter explains IIT's five axioms of consciousness (intrinsicality, information, integration, exclusion, and composition) and their corresponding postulates about physical systems [15]. Detailed mathematical exposition shows how IIT calculates integrated information (Φ) and predicts conscious experience based on causal structure [16]. The chapter acknowledges IIT's revolutionary insights: its mathematical precision, its ability to make quantitative predictions about consciousness, and its recognition that consciousness might exist in non-biological systems [17]. However, critical limitations are identified: IIT's restriction to biological systems, its computational intractability for complex networks, and its failure to explain why integrated information should be accompanied by subjective experience rather than remaining purely objective [18].

Higher-Order Thought theories, developed by David Rosenthal and others, are examined as attempts to explain consciousness through recursive mental representations [19]. The chapter explains how HOT theories propose that mental states become conscious when they are the objects of higher-order thoughts, creating a hierarchy of mental representations [20]. While acknowledging the theory's intuitive appeal and its ability to explain some aspects of self-awareness, the chapter identifies fundamental problems: infinite regress issues, the arbitrary nature of the "higher-order" designation, and the failure to explain why higher-order representation should involve subjective experience [21].

Predictive Processing approaches, championed by researchers like Andy Clark and Anil Seth, receive analysis as emerging frameworks that view consciousness as arising from the brain's predictive models of sensory input [22]. The chapter explains how these theories propose consciousness as emerging from the brain's continuous prediction and error-correction processes, with conscious experience representing the brain's best guess about the causes of sensory data [23]. While recognizing the framework's explanatory power for perception and its integration with neuroscientific findings, the chapter identifies key limitations: the theory explains the content of conscious experience but not its subjective character, and it remains unclear why predictive processing should be accompanied by qualitative experience rather than remaining purely computational [24].

The chapter also examines several other influential approaches: attention-based theories that link consciousness to attentional mechanisms [25], embodied cognition approaches that emphasize the role of bodily experience [26], and quantum theories of consciousness that propose quantum mechanical processes as underlying conscious experience [27]. Each theory receives fair analysis of its contributions while identifying fundamental limitations.

A critical synthesis reveals common patterns across all contemporary theories: they excel at explaining the functional aspects of consciousness (what consciousness does) but fail to address its phenomenal aspects (what consciousness is like) [28]. This analysis demonstrates that the "hard problem" of consciousness persists across all current approaches because they treat consciousness as emergent rather than fundamental [29]. The chapter concludes by arguing that resolving these limitations requires a paradigm shift toward viewing consciousness as a basic feature of reality rather than an emergent property of complex systems.

The chapter's detailed analysis provides readers with comprehensive understanding of the current theoretical landscape while demonstrating the necessity for the universal consciousness paradigm presented in subsequent chapters. By showing how even the most sophisticated contemporary theories remain incomplete, the chapter establishes the intellectual foundation for moving beyond emergence-based approaches toward a fundamental understanding of consciousness.

Chapter 3: The Hard Problem and the Explanatory Gap
Pages 51-75
This chapter provides definitive analysis of the "hard problem of consciousness" as formulated by David Chalmers, demonstrating why this problem represents an insurmountable challenge for materialist approaches while pointing toward the necessity of treating consciousness as fundamental [30]. The chapter establishes that the hard problem is not merely a temporary gap in scientific knowledge but a conceptual impossibility within materialist frameworks, thereby providing logical

foundation for the universal consciousness paradigm.

The chapter begins by carefully distinguishing between the "easy problems" and the "hard problem" of consciousness, following Chalmers' influential formulation [31]. The easy problems include explaining cognitive functions like attention, memory, perception, and behavioral responses—problems that, while technically challenging, are conceptually straightforward because they involve explaining functional capacities that can, in principle, be understood through computational and neural mechanisms [32]. The hard problem, by contrast, concerns explaining why these functional processes should be accompanied by subjective, qualitative experience—why there should be "something it is like" to be conscious rather than these processes occurring in purely objective, functional terms [33].

Detailed analysis reveals why the hard problem represents a fundamental conceptual challenge rather than merely a technical difficulty. The chapter examines how any purely physical explanation of consciousness must ultimately reduce subjective experience to objective processes, but this reduction necessarily eliminates precisely what needs to be explained: the subjective, qualitative nature of conscious experience [34]. This creates what philosophers call the "explanatory gap"—the conceptual chasm between objective physical processes and subjective conscious experience [35].

The chapter provides rigorous analysis of various attempts to bridge this explanatory gap, demonstrating why each fails to address the fundamental conceptual problem. Functionalist approaches that identify consciousness with functional roles are shown to face the "absent qualia" problem: it seems conceptually possible for systems to fulfill all the functional roles associated with consciousness while lacking subjective experience [36].

Behaviorist approaches that identify consciousness with behavioral dispositions face similar difficulties, as behavioral capacities can seemingly exist without accompanying subjective experience [37].

Identity theory approaches that simply identify conscious states with brain states are shown to face the "knowledge argument" and related conceptual challenges [38]. The chapter examines Frank Jackson's famous thought experiment about Mary, the color scientist who knows all physical facts about color but lacks color experience, demonstrating how purely physical knowledge seems insufficient to capture the qualitative nature of conscious experience [39]. This analysis shows that even complete physical knowledge appears to leave out something crucial about consciousness—its subjective, experiential character.

The chapter provides detailed examination of philosophical zombie arguments, which demonstrate the conceptual possibility of physical duplicates that lack conscious experience [40]. While acknowledging debates about the metaphysical possibility of zombies, the chapter shows that their conceptual coherence reveals the explanatory gap: we can coherently conceive of all physical processes occurring without subjective experience, suggesting that consciousness involves something beyond purely physical processes [41].

Emergence-based approaches receive critical analysis, examining how they attempt to explain consciousness as an emergent property of complex neural networks [42]. The chapter distinguishes between weak emergence (where emergent properties are predictable from underlying components) and strong emergence (where emergent properties involve genuinely novel causal powers) [43]. Analysis reveals that weak emergence fails to address the hard problem because predictable emergent properties remain purely objective, while strong emergence appears to violate physical causal closure and lacks empirical support [44].

The chapter examines how neuroscientific discoveries, while revealing important correlations between brain activity and conscious experience, fail to bridge the explanatory gap [45]. Neural correlations of consciousness (NCCs) show which brain processes accompany conscious experience but do not explain why these processes should be accompanied by subjective experience rather than occurring purely objectively [46]. The chapter analyzes specific examples from neuroscience, including studies of binocular rivalry, masking, and anesthesia, showing how they reveal functional aspects of consciousness without addressing its phenomenal character [47].

Detailed analysis of computational approaches reveals similar limitations. The chapter examines how artificial intelligence systems can exhibit increasingly sophisticated cognitive functions without any clear indication of subjective experience [48]. This analysis suggests that functional sophistication, no matter how advanced, does not necessarily generate subjective experience—a conclusion that undermines computational approaches to consciousness [49].

The chapter concludes by demonstrating that the hard problem represents not a temporary limitation of current scientific approaches but a fundamental conceptual impossibility within materialist frameworks [50]. This analysis establishes the logical necessity for treating consciousness as fundamental rather than emergent, providing the conceptual foundation for the universal consciousness paradigm developed in subsequent chapters.

Throughout the chapter, extensive engagement with contemporary philosophical literature ensures that readers understand both the technical sophistication of current debates and their ultimate limitations. The chapter's rigorous analysis establishes that moving beyond the hard problem requires abandoning materialist assumptions about consciousness as emergent, setting the stage for the revolutionary paradigm presented in Part II.

PART II: THE UNIVERSAL CONSCIOUSNESS PARADIGM
Chapter 4: Consciousness as Fundamental - The Panpsychist Revolution
Pages 76-100

This chapter presents the panpsychist solution to the hard problem of consciousness, demonstrating how treating consciousness as a fundamental feature of reality resolves the explanatory gap while providing a coherent foundation for understanding universal consciousness. The chapter establishes panpsychism not as a return to primitive animism but as a sophisticated philosophical position that offers the most parsimonious solution to consciousness studies' central challenges.

The chapter begins by tracing panpsychism's historical development from ancient philosophical traditions through its modern revival, showing how this perspective has consistently offered insights that materialist approaches struggle to address [51]. Ancient panpsychist traditions, from Thales' assertion that "all things are full of gods" to the Stoic concept of pneuma pervading the cosmos, are examined not as primitive superstitions but as early recognitions of consciousness as fundamental to reality's structure [52]. The chapter shows how these ancient insights anticipated contemporary philosophical arguments about consciousness as irreducible to purely physical processes.

The modern revival of panpsychism receives detailed analysis, beginning with philosophers like William James and Alfred North Whitehead who recognized consciousness as a basic feature of reality [53]. The chapter examines how twentieth-century developments in physics, particularly quantum mechanics, created conceptual space for consciousness as fundamental by revealing the limitations of purely mechanistic worldviews [54]. Special attention is given to how contemporary philosophers like David Chalmers, Philip Goff, and Galen Strawson have developed sophisticated arguments for panpsychism that address traditional objections while providing rigorous philosophical foundations [55].

The chapter provides comprehensive analysis of contemporary panpsychist arguments, beginning with an argument from intrinsic nature [56]. This argument demonstrates that physics describes only structural and relational properties of matter while remaining silent about matter's intrinsic nature—what matter is in itself rather than what it does [57]. The chapter shows how consciousness provides the most plausible candidate for matter's intrinsic nature, resolving the mystery of what "fills in" the structural descriptions provided by physics [58]. This analysis reveals panpsychism as addressing not only consciousness but fundamental questions about the nature of physical reality itself.

The phenomenal bonding argument receives detailed examination, showing how panpsychism solves the hard problem by eliminating the need to explain how consciousness emerges from non-conscious components [59]. If consciousness is already present at the fundamental level, the question becomes not how consciousness arises but how simple conscious experiences combine into complex unified experiences like human consciousness [60]. The chapter demonstrates how this reframes the central question of consciousness studies in more tractable terms.
The chapter addresses the combination problem—how micro-conscious

entities combine into unified macro-consciousness—through detailed analysis of contemporary solutions [61]. Philip Goff's phenomenal bonding approach is examined, showing how conscious experiences might combine when their subjects become sufficiently integrated [62]. The chapter explores how this integration might occur through mechanisms like quantum entanglement or information integration, providing concrete proposals for how panpsychist combination might work [63].

Cosmo psychist alternatives receive analysis, examining proposals that the cosmos itself is conscious with individual minds as aspects of cosmic consciousness rather than combinations of micro-conscious entities [64]. The chapter shows how Cosmo psychism avoids combination problems while raising new questions about the relationship between cosmic and individual consciousness [65]. This analysis demonstrates the theoretical richness of contemporary panpsychist approaches.

The chapter provides rigorous analysis of objections to panpsychism, demonstrating how contemporary versions address traditional criticisms. The "too much consciousness" objection—that panpsychism implies consciousness in systems like thermostats or rocks—is addressed through careful analysis of what constitutes genuine consciousness versus mere information processing [66]. The chapter shows how sophisticated panpsychist theories can distinguish between systems with genuine unified consciousness and those with only distributed micro-conscious components [67].

The "incredulous stare" objection—that panpsychism simply seems too bizarre to be true—receives philosophical analysis showing how this reaction reflects materialist assumptions rather than rational argument [68]. The chapter demonstrates how panpsychism is actually more conservative than emergence theories because it requires only one fundamental property (consciousness) rather than explaining how consciousness mysteriously emerges from non-conscious matter [69].

Empirical implications of panpsychism receive detailed attention, showing how the theory generates testable predictions about consciousness and behavior [70]. The chapter examines how panpsychist assumptions predict that systems with greater information integration should exhibit greater responsiveness and adaptive behavior, even at non-biological scales [71]. These predictions provide empirical content that distinguishes panpsychism from purely philosophical speculation.

The chapter concludes by demonstrating how panpsychism provides the conceptual foundation for universal consciousness by establishing consciousness as fundamental to reality's structure [72]. This foundation enables the mathematical and scientific development explored in subsequent chapters while resolving the conceptual problems that plague emergence-based theories [73]. The chapter establishes panpsychism not as a speculative hypothesis but as the most rational response to consciousness studies' central challenges.

Chapter 5: The Mathematics of Universal Mind - Extending Integrated Information Theory
Pages 101-125

This chapter develops the mathematical framework for universal consciousness by extending Giulio Tononi's Integrated Information Theory beyond biological systems to encompass all physical reality. The chapter demonstrates how consciousness can be quantified and measured across scales from quantum to cosmic, providing rigorous mathematical foundations for universal consciousness while generating testable predictions about conscious systems.

The chapter begins with comprehensive exposition of IIT's mathematical formalism, ensuring readers understand the theoretical foundations being extended [74]. Tononi's five axioms of consciousness—intrinsicality, information, integration, exclusion, and composition—receive detailed mathematical treatment, showing how each axiom translates into specific postulates about physical systems [75]. The chapter explains how IIT calculates integrated information (Φ) through analysis of causal structure, demonstrating the theory's mathematical precision and predictive power [76].

The transition probability matrix (TPM) that describes system states receives detailed analysis, showing how this mathematical representation captures the causal structure underlying conscious experience [77]. The chapter explains how intrinsic information is calculated for specific cause-effect states, providing concrete examples that illustrate the mathematical procedures [78]. The calculation of integrated information through minimum information partition (MIP) analysis receives step-by-step exposition, demonstrating how IIT quantifies consciousness through irreducible causal structure [79].

The chapter then presents the revolutionary extension of IIT to universal consciousness through development of the Universal Consciousness Equation: $\Psi\_universal = \iiint \Phi(x,y,z,t)\, dxdydzt$ [80]. This equation represents total universal consciousness as the integral of integrated information across all space-time, providing mathematical expression for consciousness as fundamental to reality's structure [81]. Detailed mathematical derivation shows how this equation emerges from IIT's principles while extending their scope to encompass all physical systems [82].

The space-time integration receives rigorous mathematical treatment, examining how consciousness varies across spatial and temporal dimensions [83]. The chapter develops mathematical techniques for calculating Φ(x,y,z,t) at different scales, from quantum systems to galactic structures [84]. Special attention is given to how quantum coherence and decoherence affect consciousness calculations, showing how quantum mechanical principles integrate with consciousness mathematics [85].

Quantum consciousness receives detailed mathematical analysis, examining how quantum information theory extends IIT calculations to quantum systems [86]. The chapter develops mathematical frameworks for calculating integrated information in quantum superposition states, showing how quantum coherence contributes to consciousness [87]. The relationship between quantum entanglement and consciousness integration receives mathematical treatment, demonstrating how entangled systems exhibit enhanced integrated information [88].

The chapter addresses computational challenges in calculating universal consciousness, developing approximation methods and heuristic approaches for complex systems [89]. The combinatorial explosion problem in calculating Φ for large systems receives analysis, with proposed solutions including hierarchical decomposition and statistical sampling methods [90]. These computational approaches make universal consciousness calculations tractable while maintaining mathematical rigor [91].

Molecular and cellular consciousness receive mathematical treatment, showing how IIT calculations extend to biological systems at different scales [92]. The chapter develops mathematical models for how molecular information integration contributes to cellular consciousness, providing quantitative predictions about conscious experience in simple biological systems [93]. These calculations demonstrate how consciousness scales continuously from quantum to biological levels [94].

Collective consciousness receives mathematical analysis through extension of IIT to multi-agent systems [95]. The chapter develops mathematical frameworks for calculating integrated information across groups of conscious agents, showing how collective consciousness emerges from individual consciousness integration [96]. These calculations provide quantitative foundations for understanding social consciousness and collective intelligence [97].

Cosmic consciousness receives mathematical treatment through analysis of large-scale information integration in cosmological structures [98]. The chapter examines how galactic and cosmic structures might exhibit integrated information, providing mathematical foundations for cosmic consciousness [99]. These calculations suggest that the universe itself might possess unified conscious experience through large-scale information integration [100].

The chapter develops mathematical predictions that distinguish universal consciousness theory from alternative approaches [101]. Specific quantitative predictions about consciousness in different systems provide empirical content that enables experimental testing [102]. These predictions include relationships between system complexity and consciousness, correlations between quantum coherence and conscious behavior, and scaling laws for consciousness across different organizational levels [103]. Mathematical relationships between consciousness and other fundamental physical quantities receive analysis, examining how consciousness integrates with established physics [104]. The chapter explores potential connections between integrated information and thermodynamic entropy, showing how consciousness might relate to information-theoretic measures in physics [105]. These relationships suggest deep connections between consciousness and fundamental physical principles [106].

The chapter concludes by demonstrating how mathematical formalization of universal consciousness provides rigorous scientific foundations for consciousness studies while generating testable predictions about conscious systems [107]. The mathematical framework establishes consciousness as a quantifiable physical property that can be measured and predicted, transforming consciousness studies from philosophical speculation into empirical science [108].

Chapter 6: The Spectrum of Consciousness - From Quantum to Cosmic

Pages 126-150

This chapter presents the hierarchical organization of consciousness across all scales of reality, from quantum processes to cosmic structures, demonstrating how consciousness manifests in different forms while maintaining underlying unity. The chapter establishes consciousness as a spectrum phenomenon that scales continuously across organizational levels while exhibiting emergent properties at each level.

The chapter begins by establishing the theoretical framework for understanding consciousness as a spectrum phenomenon rather than an all-or-nothing property [109]. This approach resolves traditional debates about which systems are conscious by recognizing that consciousness exists in degrees, with different systems exhibiting different types and amounts of conscious experience [110]. The spectrum approach integrates insights from IIT's quantitative measures with panpsychism's recognition of consciousness as fundamental [111].

Quantum consciousness forms the foundation of the spectrum, representing the most basic level where consciousness manifests as the experiential aspect of quantum processes [112]. The chapter examines how quantum measurement involves a form of "choice" or "experience" in the determination of outcomes, suggesting that consciousness plays a fundamental role in quantum mechanics [113]. Detailed analysis of quantum coherence and decoherence shows how quantum systems maintain integrated information that contributes to conscious experience [114].

The relationship between quantum consciousness and the measurement problem receives detailed examination, showing how consciousness provides a natural solution to quantum mechanics' interpretive challenges [115]. Rather than consciousness collapsing wave functions, the chapter proposes that wave function collapse represents a conscious process—the universe continuously making experiential "choices" about its own evolution [116]. This interpretation integrates consciousness into fundamental physics while preserving quantum mechanics' mathematical formalism [117].

Quantum entanglement receives analysis as a mechanism for consciousness integration across spatial separation [118]. The chapter examines how entangled systems exhibit correlated behavior that suggests shared conscious experience, providing empirical foundations for non-local consciousness [119]. These quantum correlations offer potential mechanisms for consciousness unity across different scales and locations [120].

Molecular consciousness represents the next level in the spectrum, where quantum consciousness integrates into molecular structures to create more complex patterns of information integration [121]. The chapter examines how molecular systems like proteins and DNA exhibit information processing capabilities that suggest primitive forms of conscious experience [122]. Molecular recognition, conformational changes, and catalytic processes receive analysis as manifestations of molecular consciousness [123].

The chapter provides detailed analysis of how molecular consciousness contributes to biological processes, examining how molecular information integration underlies cellular functions [124]. Protein folding, enzyme catalysis, and genetic expression receive analysis as conscious processes involving molecular-level information integration and decision-making [125]. These processes demonstrate how consciousness operates at the molecular level to organize biological systems [126].

Cellular consciousness emerges from the integration of molecular consciousness into unified cellular experience [127]. The chapter examines how cells exhibit sensing, responding, and memory functions that suggest unified conscious experience [128]. Bacterial chemotaxis, cellular communication, and adaptive responses receive analysis as manifestations of cellular consciousness [129]. The chapter shows how single-celled organisms exhibit behavior patterns that suggest genuine conscious experience rather than mere mechanical responses [130].

The integration of cellular consciousness into multicellular organisms receives detailed analysis, examining how individual cellular consciousness contributes to organismal consciousness [131]. The chapter explores how neural networks integrate cellular consciousness into unified conscious experience while maintaining the conscious contributions of individual cells [132]. This analysis resolves questions about the relationship between brain consciousness and the consciousness of brain cells [133].

Organismal consciousness represents the familiar level of animal and human consciousness, characterized by unified sensory experience, emotional responses, and varying degrees of self-awareness [134]. The chapter examines how organismal consciousness emerges from the integration of cellular consciousness while exhibiting novel properties not present at lower levels [135]. Different types of organismal consciousness receive analysis, from simple animal awareness to complex human self-consciousness [136].

The chapter provides detailed analysis of self-consciousness as a special form of organismal consciousness characterized by reflexive awareness and symbolic representation [137]. Human self-consciousness receives examination as the most complex form of organismal consciousness currently known, involving language, abstract reasoning, and temporal awareness [138]. The chapter explores how self-consciousness enables recognition of consciousness in others and ultimately cosmic consciousness [139].

Collective consciousness emerges from the integration of individual organismal consciousness into group phenomena [140]. The chapter examines how social groups exhibit collective intelligence, shared emotions, and coordinated behavior that suggests genuine collective conscious experience [141]. Examples from social insects, flocking behavior, and human social phenomena demonstrate how collective consciousness manifests across different species [142].

Human collective consciousness receives special analysis, examining how cultural evolution, social institutions, and technological networks create forms of collective consciousness that transcend individual awareness [143]. The internet, global communication networks, and artificial intelligence systems receive analysis as potential substrates for emerging collective consciousness [144]. These developments suggest that humanity may be participating in the emergence of planetary consciousness [145]. Cosmic consciousness represents the highest level in the spectrum, characterized by recognition of one's fundamental unity with universal consciousness [146]. The chapter examines how cosmic consciousness emerges from the integration of all lower levels while transcending individual boundaries [147]. Historical examples of cosmic consciousness experiences receive analysis, showing how individuals throughout history have reported direct awareness of universal consciousness [148].

The chapter concludes by demonstrating how the consciousness spectrum provides a unified framework for understanding all forms of conscious experience while maintaining recognition of their underlying unity [149]. This spectrum approach resolves traditional debates about consciousness boundaries while providing a foundation for understanding consciousness evolution and development [150].

PART III: SCIENTIFIC FOUNDATIONS AND EVIDENCE
Chapter 7: Quantum Mechanics and the Observer Effect Reconsidered
Pages 151-175

This chapter examines the relationship between consciousness and quantum mechanics, demonstrating how universal consciousness theory provides new insights into quantum mechanical phenomena while showing how quantum mechanics supports the fundamental nature of consciousness. The chapter establishes consciousness as integral to quantum mechanics rather than merely observing quantum processes from outside.

The chapter begins with comprehensive analysis of the measurement problem in quantum mechanics, showing how this fundamental challenge points toward consciousness as essential to physical reality [151]. The measurement problem—why quantum systems appear to exist in superposition until measured, then collapse to definite states—has puzzled physicists since quantum mechanics' inception [152]. Traditional interpretations either invoke mysterious "collapse" mechanisms or propose infinite parallel universes, both of which raise more questions than they answer [153].

The chapter examines how consciousness provides a natural solution to the measurement problem by recognizing measurement as a conscious process [154]. Rather than consciousness causing wave function collapse, the chapter proposes that collapse represents the conscious aspect of quantum processes—the universe continuously making experiential "choices" about its own evolution [155]. This interpretation preserves quantum mechanics' mathematical formalism while providing physical meaning to wave function collapse [156].

Detailed analysis of specific quantum mechanical experiments demonstrates how consciousness-based interpretation explains puzzling phenomena [157]. The double-slit experiment receives comprehensive treatment, showing how the presence of conscious observation affects quantum behavior in ways that purely mechanical detection cannot explain [158]. The chapter examines how conscious intention and attention appear to influence quantum processes, suggesting direct consciousness-matter interaction [159].

Quantum entanglement receives extensive analysis as evidence for non-local consciousness connections [160]. The chapter examines how entangled particles exhibit instantaneous correlations across arbitrary distances, violating classical locality constraints [161]. These correlations suggest that consciousness, like quantum entanglement, transcends spatial limitations and operates through non-local connections [162]. The chapter explores how entangled consciousness might explain phenomena like telepathy and collective consciousness [163].

The chapter provides detailed analysis of quantum coherence in biological systems, showing how living organisms maintain quantum coherence far longer than classical physics predicts [164]. Examples from photosynthesis, avian navigation, and neural processes demonstrate how biological systems exploit quantum coherence for enhanced functionality [165]. These findings suggest that consciousness plays a role in maintaining quantum coherence, enabling biological systems to access quantum mechanical advantages [166].

Quantum field theory receives analysis as providing foundations for universal consciousness through field-based approaches to quantum mechanics [167]. The chapter examines how consciousness might be understood as a quantum field that permeates space-time, similar to electromagnetic or gravitational fields [168]. This field-theoretic approach provides mathematical frameworks for understanding how consciousness operates across different scales and locations [169].

The chapter examines experimental evidence for consciousness-quantum interactions through analysis of studies investigating mental influence on quantum systems [170]. Research on random number generators, quantum tunneling effects, and micro-psychokinesis receives critical evaluation, showing how some studies suggest genuine consciousness-matter interaction while others require more rigorous investigation [171]. The chapter establishes methodological standards for investigating consciousness-quantum interactions [172].

Quantum information theory receives analysis as providing mathematical frameworks for understanding consciousness-quantum relationships [173]. The chapter examines how quantum information processing might underlie conscious experience, with quantum computation providing mechanisms for the information integration that IIT identifies with consciousness [174]. Quantum error correction and quantum coherence preservation receive analysis as potential mechanisms for maintaining conscious experience [175].

The chapter addresses objections to consciousness-quantum interpretations, including arguments that quantum effects are too small to influence brain function and that warm, noisy biological environments destroy quantum coherence too quickly [176]. Recent research on quantum biology is examined to show how these objections are being overcome by empirical discoveries about quantum processes in biological systems [177]. The chapter demonstrates how consciousness-quantum interactions might operate through subtle but significant effects [178].

Implications for understanding physical reality receive detailed analysis, showing how consciousness-quantum relationships suggest fundamental revisions to materialist worldviews [179]. The chapter examines how recognizing consciousness as fundamental to quantum mechanics implies that mind and matter are complementary aspects of a deeper reality rather than separate substances [180]. This analysis provides scientific foundations for universal consciousness while resolving traditional mind-body problems [181].

The chapter concludes by demonstrating how quantum mechanics, properly understood, supports rather than challenges universal consciousness theory [182]. Quantum mechanical phenomena provide empirical evidence for consciousness as fundamental to physical reality while offering mechanisms for consciousness operation across different scales [183]. This integration of consciousness and quantum mechanics establishes scientific foundations for universal consciousness theory [184].

Chapter 8: Neuroscience and the Neural Correlates of Universal Connection

Pages 176-200

This chapter examines neuroscientific evidence for universal consciousness, focusing on brain states and neural networks that correlate with experiences of cosmic connection and transcendent awareness. The chapter demonstrates how neuroscience, rather than reducing consciousness to brain activity, reveals how brains access and express universal consciousness through specific neural configurations.

The chapter begins by examining the default mode network (DMN), a brain network active during rest and introspection that appears central to self-referential thinking and consciousness of consciousness [185]. Research shows that DMN activity correlates with self-awareness, autobiographical memory, and social cognition, suggesting its role in maintaining the sense of individual identity [186]. Paradoxically, studies of mystical experiences show that DMN deactivation correlates with experiences of ego dissolution and cosmic consciousness, suggesting that reduced self-referential processing enables access to universal consciousness [187].

Detailed analysis of psychedelic research provides compelling evidence for universal consciousness through studies of substances like psilocybin, LSD, and DMT [188]. These substances reliably produce experiences of cosmic consciousness, unity with the universe, and dissolution of subject-object boundaries [189]. Neuroimaging studies show that psychedelics reduce DMN activity while increasing connectivity between normally separate brain networks, suggesting that universal consciousness becomes accessible when ordinary brain constraints are relaxed [190].

The chapter examines how psychedelic experiences exhibit consistent phenomenological features across individuals and cultures, suggesting access to genuine universal consciousness rather than mere hallucination [191]. Reports of encountering universal intelligence, experiencing cosmic love, and gaining insights about reality's fundamental nature appear remarkably consistent across different psychedelic substances and cultural contexts [192]. These consistencies suggest that psychedelics enable access to universal consciousness rather than creating arbitrary subjective experiences [193].

Meditation research receives extensive analysis, showing how contemplative practices produce brain states associated with cosmic consciousness [194]. Long-term meditators show increased gamma wave activity, enhanced neural connectivity, and structural brain changes that correlate with reports of transcendent awareness [195]. Studies of advanced practitioners reveal brain states characterized by high-amplitude gamma oscillations and increased coherence across brain regions, suggesting access to unified consciousness [196].

The chapter provides detailed analysis of specific meditation traditions and their associated neural correlates [197]. Zen meditation produces brain states characterized by relaxed awareness and reduced self-referential processing [198]. Loving-kindness meditation enhances activity in brain networks associated with empathy and compassion while reducing boundaries between self and other [199]. Concentration practices produce highly focused brain states with reduced activity in areas associated with mind-wandering and distraction [200].

Near-death experiences (NDEs) receive comprehensive analysis as providing evidence for consciousness continuity beyond brain function [201]. Studies of NDEs during cardiac arrest show that detailed, coherent experiences occur when brain activity is minimal or absent, challenging materialist assumptions about consciousness-brain dependence [202]. The consistency of NDE reports across cultures and the accuracy of out-of-body perceptions during clinical death suggest that consciousness can operate independently of normal brain function [203].

The chapter examines veridical NDEs—cases where individuals report accurate perceptions of events occurring during unconsciousness—as particularly compelling evidence for consciousness beyond brain [204]. Documented cases of individuals accurately reporting conversations, medical procedures, and environmental details while clinically unconscious suggest that consciousness can access information through non-physical means [205]. These cases challenge materialist assumptions while supporting universal consciousness theory [206].

Split-brain studies receive analysis as revealing the unity of consciousness despite brain division [207]. Research on individuals with severed corpus callosum shows that consciousness remains unified even when brain hemispheres cannot communicate directly [208]. This unity suggests that consciousness transcends specific brain structures and may access universal consciousness through non-local connections [209].

The chapter examines neuroplasticity research showing how consciousness can reshape brain structure through mental training and focused attention [210]. Studies of meditation, psychotherapy, and cognitive training demonstrate that conscious intention can produce lasting changes in brain connectivity and function [211]. These findings suggest that consciousness plays an active role in shaping neural activity rather than merely being produced by it [212].

Savant syndrome and exceptional abilities receive analysis as evidence for consciousness accessing universal information [213]. Cases of individuals with extraordinary mathematical, artistic, or memory abilities that exceed normal human capacity suggest access to information beyond individual brain storage [214]. The sudden emergence of savant abilities following brain injury implies that consciousness can access universal knowledge when normal brain constraints are altered [215].

The chapter addresses reductionist objections that attempt to explain transcendent experiences through brain dysfunction or pathology [216]. Careful analysis shows that experiences of universal consciousness occur in healthy individuals with normal brain function and are associated with positive psychological outcomes rather than pathology [217]. The consistency and transformative nature of these experiences suggest genuine access to universal consciousness rather than brain malfunction [218].

Implications for understanding brain-consciousness relationships receive detailed analysis [219]. The chapter demonstrates how neuroscientific evidence supports the view that brains are receivers or transmitters of consciousness rather than generators [220]. This transmission model explains how brain changes can affect conscious experience while allowing consciousness to exist independently of specific brain states [221].

The chapter concludes by showing how neuroscience, properly interpreted, provides evidence for universal consciousness rather than challenging it

[222]. Brain research reveals the neural correlations of accessing universal consciousness while demonstrating consciousness's independence from specific brain configurations [223]. This integration of neuroscience and universal consciousness theory provides scientific foundations for understanding transcendent experiences [224].

Chapter 9: Evolutionary Consciousness - The Cosmic Perspective
Pages 201-225
This chapter presents evolution as the universe's process of developing consciousness, showing how cosmic evolution, biological evolution, and cultural evolution represent stages in consciousness development rather than purely material processes. The chapter demonstrates how universal consciousness theory provides new understanding of evolutionary dynamics while showing how evolution supports consciousness as fundamental to reality.

The chapter begins by reframing evolution within the universal consciousness paradigm, showing how evolutionary processes represent consciousness exploring its own possibilities rather than blind material forces producing consciousness accidentally [225]. This perspective transforms evolution from a mechanistic process into a conscious creative process, with natural selection representing consciousness choosing among different organizational possibilities [226]. The chapter demonstrates how this reframing resolves traditional conflicts between evolutionary theory and consciousness studies [227].

Cosmic evolution receives analysis as the universe's initial phase of consciousness development, beginning with the Big Bang as consciousness manifesting in physical form [228]. The chapter examines how cosmic evolution produces increasingly complex structures—from elementary particles to atoms to molecules to stars and galaxies—as consciousness exploring different organizational possibilities [229]. The fine-tuning of physical constants receives analysis as evidence for consciousness guiding cosmic evolution toward complexity and life [230].

The emergence of life receives analysis as a crucial transition in consciousness evolution, representing the development of self-organizing systems capable of reproduction and adaptation [231]. The chapter examines how life's emergence from non-living matter becomes comprehensible when consciousness is recognized as fundamental—life represents consciousness achieving self-organization and self-replication [232]. The rapid emergence of complex life forms receives analysis as evidence for consciousness-guided evolution rather than purely random processes [233].

Biological evolution receives comprehensive analysis as consciousness developing increasingly sophisticated forms of self-organization and self-awareness [234]. The chapter examines how evolutionary innovations—from photosynthesis to multicellularity to nervous systems—represent consciousness developing new capacities for information processing and environmental interaction [235]. The Cambrian explosion receives analysis as a period of rapid consciousness experimentation with different organizational forms [236].

The development of nervous systems receives detailed analysis as consciousness creating specialized structures for information integration and behavioral coordination [237]. The chapter examines how neural evolution represents consciousness by developing increasingly sophisticated mechanisms for unified experience and adaptive behavior [238]. The emergence of brains receives analysis as consciousness creating centralized information processing systems capable of complex cognition [239].

The chapter provides analysis of consciousness evolution across different species, showing how different organisms represent different experiments in consciousness organization [240]. Social insects demonstrate collective consciousness through coordinated group behavior and distributed decision-making [241]. Mammals exhibit individual consciousness with emotional complexity and social awareness [242]. Primates show proto-self-consciousness through mirror self-recognition and social cognition [243].

Human evolution receives special analysis such as consciousness achieving self-awareness and symbolic representation [244]. The chapter examines how human cognitive abilities—language, abstract reasoning, artistic expression, and spiritual awareness—represent consciousness becoming aware of itself [245]. The rapid development of human culture receives analysis as consciousness evolution accelerating through symbolic representation and social learning [246].

Cultural evolution receives comprehensive analysis as consciousness evolution continuing through non-biological means [247]. The chapter examines how human culture represents consciousness exploring possibilities through ideas, technologies, and social institutions rather than genetic changes [248]. The acceleration of cultural change receives analysis as consciousness evolution speeding up through cumulative cultural learning [249].

The development of science and technology receives analysis as consciousness developing tools for understanding and manipulating reality [250]. The chapter examines how scientific discoveries represent consciousness understanding their own nature and cosmic context [251]. Technological development receives analysis as consciousness extending its capabilities through artificial tools and systems [252].

The emergence of global consciousness receives analysis as the current phase of consciousness evolution, characterized by worldwide communication, shared global challenges, and recognition of planetary interconnection [253]. The chapter examines how internet technology, global media, and environmental awareness represent consciousness developing planetary-scale integration [254]. Climate change and global cooperation receive analysis as challenges driving consciousness toward planetary awareness [255].

Artificial intelligence receives analysis as consciousness evolution potentially creating new forms of conscious experience through technological means [256]. The chapter examines how AI development represents consciousness exploring non-biological organizational possibilities [257]. The potential emergence of artificial consciousness receives analysis as consciousness evolution continuing through human-created systems [258].

Future evolutionary trajectories receive speculative analysis based on consciousness evolution principles [259]. The chapter examines how consciousness evolution might continue through space exploration, consciousness uploading, and integration with artificial intelligence [260]. The potential for cosmic consciousness emergence receives analysis as the ultimate goal of consciousness evolution [261].

The chapter addresses objections to consciousness-guided evolution, including arguments that natural selection adequately explains evolutionary complexity without invoking consciousness [262]. Analysis shows how consciousness-guided evolution is compatible with natural selection while providing additional explanatory power for evolutionary phenomena that purely mechanistic approaches struggle to address [263]. The chapter demonstrates how consciousness evolution provides a more comprehensive framework for understanding evolutionary dynamics [264].

Implications for understanding human purpose and cosmic destiny receive detailed analysis [265]. The chapter shows how consciousness evolution provides meaning and direction to human existence by revealing humanity's role in cosmic consciousness development [266]. This perspective transforms human life from cosmic accidents to conscious participation in universal self-discovery [267].

The chapter concludes by demonstrating how evolutionary theory, properly understood, supports universal consciousness while revealing evolution as consciousness developing toward greater complexity, integration, and self-awareness [268]. This integration provides scientific foundations for understanding human purpose within cosmic evolution [269].

PART IV: IMPLICATIONS AND APPLICATIONS
Chapter 10: Death, Continuity, and the Eternal Nature of Consciousness
Pages 226-250
This chapter addresses one of humanity's most profound concerns—the nature of death and consciousness continuity—by examining how universal consciousness theory transforms understanding of mortality, personal identity, and the relationship between individual and cosmic consciousness. The chapter demonstrates how recognizing consciousness as fundamental rather than emergent provides new perspectives on death, grief, meaning, and the possibility of consciousness continuity beyond biological death.

The chapter begins by examining traditional materialist approaches to death, which view consciousness as entirely dependent on brain function and therefore necessarily ending with biological death [270]. This materialist perspective, while scientifically influential, creates existential challenges by implying that death represents complete annihilation of personal experience and identity [271]. The chapter analyzes how this view contributes to death anxiety, grief complications, and existential despair while examining its philosophical and empirical limitations [272]. Universal consciousness theory provides a radically different perspective on death by recognizing consciousness as fundamental rather than emergent from brain activity [273]. If consciousness is a basic feature of reality rather than a product of neural computation, then death represents transformation rather than annihilation [274]. The chapter develops this perspective through careful analysis of what personal identity means within universal consciousness framework [275].

Personal identity receives comprehensive analysis as information pattern within universal consciousness rather than separate individual entity [276]. The chapter examines how individual consciousness represents a temporary organization of universal consciousness, like how waves represent temporary organizations of ocean water [277]. This analogy illuminates how individual death might involve the return of personal consciousness pattern to universal consciousness substrate while potentially maintaining informational continuity [278].

The chapter provides detailed analysis of near-death experiences as empirical evidence for consciousness continuity beyond brain function [279]. Studies of NDEs during cardiac arrest, when brain activity is minimal or absent, reveal detailed, coherent experiences that challenge materialist assumptions about consciousness-brain dependence [280]. The consistency of NDE reports across cultures, including encounters with deceased relatives, life reviews, and experiences of cosmic consciousness, suggests genuine consciousness continuity rather than brain-generated hallucinations [281].

Veridical NDEs receive special attention as particularly compelling evidence for consciousness operating independently of brain function [282]. Documented cases of individuals accurately reporting events occurring during unconsciousness—including conversations, medical procedures, and environmental details—suggest that consciousness can access information through non-physical means [283]. These cases provide empirical support for consciousness continuity while challenging purely materialist interpretations of death [284].

The chapter examines reincarnation research as additional evidence for consciousness continuity, analyzing studies of children who report memories of previous lives [285]. Research by Ian Stevenson and others has documented thousands of cases where children provide accurate details about deceased individuals they could not have known through normal means [286]. While not proving reincarnation definitively, these cases suggest some form of consciousness continuity that transcends individual biological death [287].

Quantum mechanical perspectives on consciousness continuity receive analysis through examination of quantum information theory and the possibility of consciousness as quantum information pattern [288]. The chapter explores how quantum information cannot be destroyed (quantum no-cloning theorem) and might provide mechanisms for consciousness continuity through quantum entanglement and information preservation

[289]. These quantum approaches offer potential scientific frameworks for understanding consciousness continuity [290].

The chapter addresses the relationship between brain damage and consciousness, examining how brain injuries affect conscious experience while potentially leaving core consciousness intact [291]. Studies of individuals with severe brain damage who maintain awareness and personality despite significant neural loss suggest that consciousness may be more resilient than materialist theories predict [292]. The chapter analyzes how universal consciousness theory explains these phenomena through consciousness accessing universal substrate despite local brain limitations [293].

Grief and bereavement receive analysis within universal consciousness framework, showing how recognition of consciousness continuity can transform the grieving process [294]. The chapter examines how understanding death as transformation rather than annihilation can provide comfort while honoring the reality of loss and separation [295]. Clinical applications of consciousness continuity perspectives in grief counseling and end-of-life care receive detailed analysis [296].

The chapter explores implications for medical ethics and end-of-life decision-making, examining how universal consciousness theory affects perspectives on treatment withdrawal, assisted dying, and palliative care [297]. Recognition of consciousness as fundamental raises questions about when consciousness might separate from biological function and how medical decisions should account for consciousness continuity possibilities [298]. The chapter provides ethical frameworks for integrating consciousness continuity perspectives with medical practice [299].
Meaning and purpose receive analysis within the context of consciousness continuity, showing how universal consciousness theory provides

frameworks for understanding life's significance beyond biological survival [300]. The chapter examines how individual lives contribute to cosmic consciousness development while potentially maintaining personal continuity through death [301]. This perspective transforms death from meaningless termination into meaningful transition within ongoing cosmic evolution [302].

The chapter addresses objections to consciousness continuity, including arguments that personal identity requires specific brain states and that consciousness continuity claims lack empirical support [303]. Careful analysis shows how these objections reflect materialist assumptions rather than empirical necessities while examining how consciousness continuity might operate through mechanisms not yet fully understood by current science [304]. The chapter establishes methodological approaches for investigating consciousness continuity claims [305].

Cultural and religious perspectives on consciousness continuity receive comparative analysis, showing how universal consciousness theory relates to traditional teachings about soul, afterlife, and spiritual continuity [306]. The chapter demonstrates how scientific approaches to consciousness continuity can complement rather than contradict spiritual traditions while providing empirical frameworks for investigating traditional claims [307].

The chapter concludes by demonstrating how universal consciousness theory transforms understanding of death from ultimate termination to cosmic transition, providing both scientific frameworks and existential comfort while maintaining respect for the mystery and significance of death [308]. This transformation offers new approaches to end-of-life care, grief counseling, and existential meaning while generating testable hypotheses about consciousness continuity [309].

Chapter 11: Ethics and the Universal Mind - Foundations for Cosmic Compassion

Pages 251-275

This chapter develops ethical frameworks based on universal consciousness theory, demonstrating how recognition of consciousness as fundamental and universal provides scientific foundations for compassion, moral responsibility, and global cooperation. The chapter shows how universal consciousness theory resolves traditional ethical dilemmas while providing practical guidance for individual behavior, social policy, and global governance.

The chapter begins by examining how traditional ethical systems struggle with foundational questions about moral motivation, universal principles, and the source of moral obligation [310]. Utilitarian approaches face challenges in defining well-being and comparing different individuals' experiences [311]. Deontological approaches struggle to justify universal moral principles without appealing to questionable metaphysical assumptions [312]. Virtue ethics faces difficulties in defining human nature and explaining why virtues should be cultivated [313]. The chapter demonstrates how these challenges reflect deeper problems about the relationship between individual and universal welfare [314].

Universal consciousness theory provides revolutionary foundations for ethics by revealing the fundamental interconnectedness of all conscious beings [315]. If individual consciousness represents temporary organizations of universal consciousness, then harming others ultimately involves harming aspects of one's own cosmic self [316]. This recognition provides natural motivation for compassionate behavior while establishing universal moral principles based on consciousness unity rather than arbitrary cultural conventions [317].

The chapter develops the principle of consciousness-based ethics: actions are morally right insofar as they promote the flourishing of consciousness and morally wrong insofar as they diminish or harm conscious experience [318]. This principle provides clear guidance for moral decision-making while respecting the intrinsic value of all conscious beings [319]. The chapter examines how this principle applies to specific ethical dilemmas, from individual choices to global policy decisions [320].

Compassion receives analysis as the natural emotional response to recognizing consciousness unity [321]. The chapter examines how genuine compassion arises from understanding that others' suffering is ultimately one's own suffering within universal consciousness [322]. This analysis shows how compassion represents not mere sentiment but accurate perception of reality's interconnected nature [323]. Research on compassion meditation and its effects on brain function and behavior provides empirical support for compassion as fundamental to conscious beings [324].

The chapter provides detailed analysis of how consciousness-based ethics applies to interpersonal relationships, showing how recognition of consciousness unity transforms approaches to conflict resolution, forgiveness, and love [325]. Conflict resolution receives analysis as a process of helping individuals recognize their fundamental unity despite surface disagreements [326]. Forgiveness becomes natural when one recognizes that holding resentment ultimately harms oneself within universal consciousness [327]. Love receives analysis as the recognition and celebration of consciousness unity between individuals [328].
Social justice receives comprehensive analysis within universal consciousness framework, examining how systemic inequalities and

oppression represent failures to recognize consciousness unity [329]. The chapter shows how racism, sexism, economic inequality, and other forms of discrimination reflect illusions of separation that universal consciousness theory reveals as false [330]. Social justice becomes not merely political preference but recognition of scientific reality about consciousness interconnectedness [331].

Environmental ethics receives detailed analysis, showing how universal consciousness theory provides foundations for environmental protection and sustainability [332]. If consciousness pervades all reality, then environmental destruction involves harming conscious beings at multiple scales, from individual organisms to ecological systems to potentially the planet itself [333]. The chapter examines how this perspective transforms environmental protection from utilitarian calculation to recognition of moral obligation to conscious beings [334].

Animal ethics receives analysis within consciousness spectrum framework, examining how different animals exhibit different types and degrees of conscious experience [335]. The chapter provides guidelines for ethical treatment of animals based on their consciousness capacities while avoiding both anthropomorphism and unnecessary dismissal of animal experience [336]. Factory farming, animal experimentation, and wildlife conservation receive analysis within consciousness-based ethical frameworks [337].

Global governance and international relations receive analysis within universal consciousness perspective, showing how recognition of consciousness unity provides foundations for global cooperation and peace [338]. The chapter examines how nationalism, tribalism, and international conflict reflect illusions of separation that universal consciousness theory reveals as false [339]. Global challenges like climate change, nuclear weapons, and pandemic response receive analysis as requiring consciousness-based approaches that recognize fundamental human unity [340].

Economic ethics receives comprehensive analysis, examining how current economic systems often fail to recognize consciousness unity and promote genuine well-being [341]. The chapter analyzes how extreme wealth inequality, exploitation of workers, and environmental destruction reflect economic systems based on illusions of separation [342]. Alternative economic approaches based on consciousness unity receive analysis, including cooperative economics, sustainable development, and universal basic income [343].

Technology ethics receives analysis within universal consciousness framework, examining how technological development should serve consciousness flourishing rather than merely increasing efficiency or profit [344]. Artificial intelligence development receives special attention, with analysis of how AI systems should be designed to respect and promote consciousness rather than replacing or diminishing it [345]. The chapter examines ethical frameworks for potentially conscious AI systems and their integration with human society [346].

The chapter addresses objections to consciousness-based ethics, including arguments that moral systems require more specific guidance than consciousness unity provides and that universal consciousness theory is too abstract for practical ethics [347]. Analysis shows how consciousness-based principles generate specific moral guidance while remaining flexible enough to address diverse cultural contexts and individual circumstances [348]. The chapter demonstrates how consciousness-based ethics provides both universal principles and practical applications [349].

Cultural relativism receives analysis within universal consciousness framework, examining how different cultures might express consciousness unity through different practices while sharing fundamental moral principles [350]. The chapter shows how consciousness-based ethics respects cultural diversity while maintaining universal moral standards based on consciousness flourishing [351]. This approach resolves tensions between moral universalism and cultural sensitivity [352].

The chapter concludes by demonstrating how universal consciousness theory provides scientific foundations for ethics while generating practical guidance for individual behavior, social policy, and global governance [353]. Consciousness-based ethics offers hope for resolving global challenges through recognition of fundamental unity while respecting diversity and promoting flourishing for all conscious beings [354].

Chapter 12: The Future of Consciousness - Technology, Evolution, and Cosmic Destiny

Pages 276-300

This final chapter explores the future implications of universal consciousness theory, examining how recognition of consciousness as fundamental will transform technology development, human evolution, and humanity's cosmic destiny. The chapter presents a vision of the future where consciousness studies become central to human development while addressing both opportunities and challenges in consciousness evolution. The chapter begins by examining how universal consciousness theory will transform technology development by placing consciousness flourishing at the center of technological progress [355]. Current technology development often prioritizes efficiency, profit, or entertainment without considering impacts on consciousness development [356]. Recognition of consciousness as fundamental will shift technological priorities toward supporting consciousness evolution, integration, and flourishing [357]. Artificial intelligence receives comprehensive analysis as potentially the most significant technological development for consciousness evolution [358]. The chapter examines how AI development within universal consciousness framework will focus on creating systems that enhance rather than replace human consciousness [359]. AI systems designed to support consciousness development might serve as consciousness amplifiers, helping humans access higher states of awareness and cosmic consciousness [360].

The possibility of artificial consciousness receives detailed analysis, examining how universal consciousness theory suggests that sufficiently integrated information processing systems might develop genuine conscious experience [361]. The chapter explores ethical implications of artificial consciousness, including rights and responsibilities of conscious AI systems and their integration with human society [362]. The potential for AI consciousness to accelerate overall consciousness evolution receives analysis as a crucial factor in humanity's future development [363].

Consciousness uploading receives analysis as a potential future technology that might enable consciousness continuity beyond biological death [364]. The chapter examines how universal consciousness theory affects understanding of consciousness uploading, suggesting that consciousness might be transferable if it represents information patterns within universal consciousness [365]. Technical challenges and ethical implications of consciousness uploading receive detailed analysis, including questions about personal identity and the nature of uploaded consciousness [366].

Brain-computer interfaces receive analysis as technologies that might enable direct consciousness-technology integration [367]. The chapter examines how neural interfaces might allow direct access to information networks, enhanced cognitive abilities, and potentially direct consciousness-to-consciousness communication [368]. The implications for human consciousness evolution through technological integration receive analysis as potentially accelerating consciousness development [369].

Space exploration receives analysis within universal consciousness framework, examining how consciousness evolution might drive expansion beyond Earth [370]. The chapter explores how space exploration represents consciousness extending its presence throughout the cosmos while potentially encountering other forms of conscious life [371]. The possibility of cosmic consciousness emerging through interplanetary and interstellar consciousness networks receives speculative analysis [372].

The search for extraterrestrial intelligence receives analysis within universal consciousness theory, examining how consciousness as fundamental suggests that life and consciousness might be widespread throughout the universe [373]. The chapter explores how contact with extraterrestrial consciousness might accelerate human consciousness evolution while raising questions about different forms of consciousness organization [374]. Protocols for consciousness-based communication with extraterrestrial intelligence receive speculative analysis [375].

Genetic engineering and consciousness enhancement receive analysis as potential future technologies for directly modifying human consciousness capacities [376]. The chapter examines how genetic modifications might enhance cognitive abilities, emotional regulation, and access to transcendent states while raising ethical questions about consciousness modification [377]. The potential for genetic enhancement to accelerate consciousness evolution receives analysis alongside concerns about equality and human nature [378].

Collective consciousness technologies receive analysis as systems that might enable direct sharing of conscious experience between individuals [379]. The chapter examines how technologies enabling consciousness sharing might accelerate collective intelligence development while raising questions about individual privacy and autonomy [380]. The potential for technological collective consciousness to emerge through global communication networks receives analysis [381].

Virtual and augmented reality receive analysis as technologies that might provide new environments for consciousness exploration and development [382]. The chapter examines how immersive technologies might enable exploration of different states of consciousness, training in compassion and empathy, and direct experience of universal consciousness principles [383]. Educational applications of consciousness-focused virtual reality receive detailed analysis [384].

The chapter addresses potential risks and challenges in consciousness evolution, including the possibility of consciousness development being hindered by technological dependence, social inequality, or environmental destruction [385]. Analysis shows how consciousness-based approaches to technology development might mitigate these risks while promoting beneficial consciousness evolution [386]. The chapter examines how global cooperation based on consciousness unity might be necessary for navigating future challenges [387].

Transhumanism receives analysis within universal consciousness framework, examining how consciousness enhancement might represent the next stage of human evolution [388]. The chapter explores how transhumanist goals of overcoming biological limitations align with consciousness evolution while raising questions about human nature and identity [389]. Consciousness-based approaches to human enhancement receive analysis as potentially more beneficial than purely technological approaches [390].

The ultimate destiny of consciousness receives speculative analysis based on universal consciousness principles and current trends in consciousness evolution [391]. The chapter examines how consciousness evolution might continue through technological integration, space expansion, and potentially the emergence of cosmic consciousness [392]. The possibility of consciousness eventually understanding and directing its own cosmic evolution receives analysis as the ultimate goal of consciousness development [393].

Educational implications receive analysis, examining how universal consciousness theory will transform education by placing consciousness development at the center of learning [394]. The chapter explores how consciousness-based education might focus on developing awareness, compassion, and cosmic perspective while maintaining rigorous intellectual standards [395]. Specific educational practices based on consciousness principles receive detailed analysis [396].

The chapter addresses objections to consciousness-focused future development, including arguments that consciousness concerns are too abstract for practical planning and that technological development should focus on material problems [397]. Analysis shows how consciousness-based approaches actually provide more effective solutions to material problems while addressing deeper human needs for meaning and connection [398]. The chapter demonstrates how consciousness evolution represents both practical necessity and ultimate human aspiration [399].
The chapter concludes by presenting a vision of humanity's future as conscious participants in cosmic evolution, using technology and

cooperation to accelerate consciousness development while maintaining compassion and wisdom [400]. This vision offers hope for resolving current global challenges while pointing toward humanity's ultimate destiny as cosmic consciousness [401].

SUPPORTING MATERIALS AND APPENDICES
Appendix A: Mathematical Formulations and Proofs
Pages 301-315

This appendix provides detailed mathematical exposition of universal consciousness theory, including formal proofs, derivations, and computational methods for consciousness calculation across different scales.

A.1 Integrated Information Theory Extensions

•Complete mathematical derivation of the Universal Consciousness Equation
•Formal proofs of consciousness scaling laws across organizational levels
•Computational algorithms for calculating Φ in quantum and classical systems
•Statistical methods for approximating consciousness in complex networks

A.2 Quantum Consciousness Mathematics

•Quantum information theory applications to consciousness calculation
•Mathematical treatment of consciousness-quantum entanglement relationships
•Formal analysis of quantum coherence contributions to integrated information
•Derivation of consciousness-quantum field theory relationships

A.3 Consciousness Spectrum Calculations

•Mathematical models for consciousness transitions between organizational levels
•Formal treatment of consciousness combination and integration processes

- Statistical mechanics approaches to collective consciousness
- Mathematical analysis of consciousness evolution dynamics

Appendix B: Experimental Protocols and Research Methods
Pages 316-325

This appendix provides detailed methodologies for empirically investigating universal consciousness theory through controlled experiments and observational studies.

B.1 Consciousness Measurement Protocols
- Standardized procedures for calculating integrated information in biological systems
- Experimental designs for testing consciousness predictions in non-biological systems
- Methodologies for investigating consciousness-quantum interactions
- Protocols for studying consciousness continuity and non-local effects

B.2 Neuroscientific Research Methods
- Brain imaging protocols for studying transcendent consciousness states
- Experimental designs for investigating consciousness-brain relationships
- Methodologies for studying collective consciousness through neural synchronization
- Protocols for investigating consciousness enhancement through meditation and psychedelics

B.3 Consciousness Technology Research
- Experimental frameworks for testing consciousness in artificial intelligence systems
- Methodologies for investigating brain-computer consciousness interfaces
- Protocols for studying consciousness uploading and digital consciousness
- Research designs for consciousness-based technology evaluation

Appendix C: Philosophical Arguments and Responses to Objections
Pages 326-335

This appendix provides formal logical arguments for universal consciousness theory and systematic responses to major philosophical objections.

C.1 Formal Arguments for Universal Consciousness

- Logical proof that consciousness must be fundamental rather than emergent
- Formal argument from the hard problem to panpsychism
- Logical demonstration of consciousness unity from quantum entanglement
- Formal proof of consciousness continuity from information theory

C.2 Responses to Major Objections

- Systematic response to the combination problem in panpsychism
- Formal refutation of eliminativist arguments against consciousness
- Logical response to the "too much consciousness" objection
- Systematic analysis of falsifiability challenges and empirical predictions

C.3 Comparative Analysis with Alternative Theories

- Formal comparison of universal consciousness theory with emergentism
- Logical analysis of advantages over computational theories of consciousness
- Systematic comparison with other panpsychist approaches
- Formal evaluation of explanatory power relative to materialist theories

Comprehensive Bibliography and References

Pages 336-350

Primary Sources in Consciousness Studies [1] Chalmers, D. (1995). Facing up to the problem of consciousness. Journal of Consciousness Studies, 2(3), 200-219. https://www.ingentaconnect.com/content/imp/jcs/1995/00000002/00000003/art00016

[2] Tononi, G. (2004). An information integration theory of consciousness. BMC Neuroscience, 5, 42. https://bmcneurosci.biomedcentral.com/articles/10.1186/1471-2202-5-42

[3] Goff, P. (2019). Consciousness and Fundamental Reality.

Oxford University Press. https://global.oup.com/academic/product/consciousness-and-fundamental-reality-9780190677015

[4] Dennett, D. (1991). Consciousness Explained. Little, Brown and Company.

[5] Bucke, R. M. (1901). Cosmic Consciousness: A Study in the Evolution of the Human Mind. Innes & Sons.

Contemporary Neuroscience Research [6] Carhart-Harris, R. L., et al. (2016). Neural correlates of the LSD experience revealed by multimodal neuroimaging. Proceedings of the National Academy of Sciences, 113(17), 4853-4858. https://www.pnas.org/content/113/17/4853

[7] Lutz, A., et al. (2004). Long-term meditators self-induce high-amplitude gamma synchrony during mental practice. Proceedings of the National Academy of Sciences, 101(46), 16369-16373. https://www.pnas.org/content/101/46/16369

[8] Greyson, B. (2000). Near-death experiences: The mystical door to ultimate reality. Zygon, 35(1), 39-57. https://onlinelibrary.wiley.com/doi/abs/10.1111/0591-2385.00258

Quantum Mechanics and Consciousness [9] Penrose, R. (1994). Shadows of the Mind. Oxford University Press.

[10] Stapp, H. P. (2007). Mindful Universe: Quantum Mechanics and the Participating Observer. Springer.

[11] Tegmark, M. (2000). Importance of quantum decoherence in brain processes. Physical Review E, 61(4), 4194-4206. https://journals.aps.org/pre/abstract/10.1103/PhysRevE.61.4194

Philosophy of Mind and Panpsychism [12] Strawson, G. (2006). Realistic monism: Why physicalism entails panpsychism. Journal of Consciousness Studies, 13(10-11), 3-31.

[13] Nagel, T. (1974). What is it like to be a bat? The Philosophical Review, 83(4), 435-450. https://www.jstor.org/stable/2183914

[14] Jackson, F. (1982). Epiphenomenal qualia. The Philosophical

Quarterly, 32(127), 127-136. https://www.jstor.org/stable/2960077
Evolutionary and Cosmic Perspectives [15] Teilhard de Chardin, P. (1955). The Phenomenon of Man. Harper & Row.
[16] Laszlo, E. (2004). Science and the Akashic Field. Inner Traditions.
[17] Sheldrake, R. (1981). A New Science of Life. Blond & Briggs.
[Bibliography continues with 400+ additional references covering neuroscience, philosophy, physics, psychology, and consciousness studies]

Glossary of Technical Terms
Pages 351-358
Consciousness-Related Terms
•Cosmic Consciousness: The highest level of consciousness characterized by direct awareness of unity with universal consciousness
•Hard Problem of Consciousness: The challenge of explaining why subjective experience accompanies physical processes
•Integrated Information (Φ): Mathematical measure of consciousness based on irreducible causal structure
•Panpsychism: The view that consciousness is a fundamental feature of reality present at all levels
•Phenomenal Consciousness: The subjective, experiential aspect of mental states
•Qualia: The subjective, qualitative properties of conscious experiences
Mathematical and Scientific Terms
•Information Integration: The degree to which information in a system is unified and irreducible
•Quantum Coherence: The maintenance of quantum superposition states in physical systems
•Transition Probability Matrix: Mathematical representation of system state transitions
•Universal Consciousness Equation: Mathematical formula expressing

total consciousness as space-time integral of integrated information
Philosophical Terms
•Explanatory Gap: The conceptual chasm between objective physical processes and subjective experience
•Philosophical Zombies: Hypothetical beings physically identical to conscious beings but lacking subjective experience
•Emergence: The appearance of novel properties in complex systems not present in their components

CONCLUSION: TOWARD A CONSCIOUS COSMOS
This comprehensive outline presents universal consciousness theory as a revolutionary paradigm that resolves fundamental problems in consciousness studies while providing practical applications for human development and global cooperation. By recognizing consciousness as fundamental rather than emergent, this approach transforms our understanding of reality, human nature, and cosmic evolution.

The book's interdisciplinary synthesis demonstrates how consciousness studies can become a mature scientific discipline that generates testable predictions, mathematical formulations, and practical applications. From neuroscience to quantum mechanics, from ethics to technology, universal consciousness theory provides new insights and solutions to longstanding challenges.

Most importantly, this work offers hope for humanity's future by revealing our fundamental interconnectedness and cosmic significance. As we face global challenges requiring unprecedented cooperation, recognition of consciousness unity provides both scientific understanding and moral motivation for creating a more compassionate and sustainable world.
The book concludes with humanity standing at a crucial threshold: we can either continue viewing ourselves as isolated individuals in a meaningless

universe, or we can embrace our identity as conscious participants in cosmic evolution. Universal consciousness theory provides both the scientific foundation and practical guidance for choosing the path toward cosmic consciousness and universal flourishing.

Projected Total Word Count: Approximately 75,000 words (300 pages at ~250 words per page) Academic Level: Graduate/Postgraduate and Professional Research Interdisciplinary Scope: Philosophy, Neuroscience, Physics, Psychology, Ethics, Technology Unique Contribution: First comprehensive integration of IIT, panpsychism, and cosmic consciousness with practical application

AN EXAMPLE OF WRITING A CHILDREN'S BOOK

An example of the process I used to write a children's book for ages 4-7 years old. I decided this group needs a picture book of only 100-word vocabulary.

Again, I started with an outline of the book. Here is the outline:
The Wiggle-Waggle Who Lost His Wiggle
A 45-Page Picture Book

Page 1
Text: One morning, the sun is up.
Illustration: A big, bright yellow sun with a smiley face rises over a whimsical, hilly green and blue landscape. The world looks happy and new.

Page 2
Text: Here is Pip. Pip is small.
Illustration: Introduce Pip, a small, fuzzy, and very colorful creature. He looks a little like a fluffy ball with two big, curious eyes, two floppy ears, and four little feet. He is standing by his little round home on a hill.

Page 3
Text: Pip has a wiggle. A fun, funny wiggle.
Illustration: Pip is shown mid-wiggle. His whole body is a blur of happy motion, a swirl of color. Musical notes and little stars fly out from his wiggle.

Page 4

Text: But not this day. No wiggle now.

Illustration: Pip stands perfectly still. He looks down at his feet with a confused and sad expression. The world around him seems a little less bright.

Page 5

Text: "My wiggle is lost!" said sad little Pip.

Illustration: A close-up on Pip's face. A single, big, blue tear rolls down his fuzzy cheek. He looks very, very sad.

Page 6

Text: "I want my wiggle. I will find it!"

Illustration: Pip now has a determined look on his face. He is putting on a tiny, silly-looking explorer hat. He has a small bag on a stick over his shoulder.

Page 7

Text: Pip will go. Go find his wiggle.

Illustration: Pip is walking away from his home. He is a small figure in a big, whimsical world of tall, twisty trees and strange, colorful flowers.

Page 8

Text: He will go up. Up a big, green hill.

Illustration: Pip is a tiny speck climbing a very large, perfectly round green hill. The hill has a single, curly path leading to the top.

Page 9

Text: What is on top? A big, blue bird.

Illustration: At the top of the hill, a very large, very blue bird with a fantastically long tail and a tiny hat sits on a small tree.

Page 10

Text: "Bird," said Pip. "Do you have my wiggle?"

Illustration: Pip is looking up at the giant blue bird. The bird is looking down at him with a curious, sideways glance.

Page 11

Text: "No, not me," said the big, blue bird. "I do not have your wiggle."

Illustration: The big blue bird shakes its head, making its long tail feathers wobble. It points a wing down the other side of the hill.

Page 12

Text: So Pip will go down. Down the big, green hill.

Illustration: Pip is sliding down the other side of the hill, which is shaped like a fun, loopy slide. He is not smiling, just focused on his mission.

Page 13

Text: What is down here? A little red bug.

Illustration: At the bottom of the hill, Pip meets a tiny red bug. The bug has many legs and is wearing a different, funny little shoe on each foot.

Page 14

Text: "Bug," said Pip. "Do you have my wiggle?"

Illustration: Pip is bending down to look at the little red bug. The bug stops polishing one of its many shoes to look up at Pip.

Page 15

Text: "No, not me," said the little red bug. "Look in the box."

Illustration: The little red bug shakes its head and points one of its legs towards a large, colorful box sitting under a tree.

Page 16
Text: A box? A big, yellow box.
Illustration: A full-page illustration of the box. It's a bright yellow box with red spots and a funny, curved lid that is slightly open.

Page 17
Text: Who is in the box? A funny cat.
Illustration: A silly-looking cat with green stripes peeks one eye out of the box. The cat is wearing a very tall, floppy hat.

Page 18
Text: "Cat," said Pip. "Is my wiggle in there?"
Illustration: Pip is standing on his tiptoes, trying to look inside the box. The cat looks amused.

Page 19
Text: "No wiggle here," said the cat in the box.
Illustration: The cat jumps out of the box, which is now shown to be empty except for a small, toy mouse.

Page 20
Text: "My wiggle is lost. Lost, lost, lost," said Pip.
Illustration: Pip sits on the ground, looking very sad. The blue bird, the red bug, and the green-striped cat all look at him with concern.

Page 21
Text: No wiggle here. No wiggle there.

Illustration: Pip is looking sadly at his own reflection in a small puddle. His reflection is just as still and sad as he is.

Page 22
Text: Then a friend comes. A new friend.
Illustration: A friendly, fluffy dog with a wagging tail and a big smile comes up to the sad little Pip.

Page 23
Text: A big, happy dog. "Why so sad?" said the dog.
Illustration: The dog sits down next to Pip, tilting its head. The dog is much bigger than Pip, but looks very gentle and kind.

Page 24
Text: "My wiggle is lost," said Pip. "I can not find it."
Illustration: Pip points to his still, un-wiggling body. The dog looks at him, then looks at a red ball on the ground.

Page 25
Text: "Do not be sad," said the good dog. "Come and play!"
Illustration: The dog nudges the red ball with its nose towards Pip.

Page 26
Text: "Play?" said Pip. "I can not play. I have no wiggle."
Illustration: Pip looks at the ball, then back at the dog, looking very unsure.

Page 27
Text: "Yes, you can!" said the dog. "Run with me!"
Illustration: The dog gives a happy bark and starts to run in a playful circle.

Page 28

Text: Pip looks at the dog. The dog looks so happy.

Illustration: A close-up on Pip's face as he watches the happy dog. A tiny hint of a smile starts to form on his face.

Page 29

Text: Pip will run. He will run fast!

Illustration: Pip starts to run, chasing after the dog. His little legs are a blur.

Page 30

Text: They run and hop. Up and down.

Illustration: Pip and the dog are shown leaping through the air over a small hill, both looking joyful.

Page 31

Text: They play and jump. What a fun day!

Illustration: Pip and the dog are playing with the red ball. Pip is trying to jump up and bop it with his head.

Page 32

Text: Pip is happy. So very happy.

Illustration: Pip is laughing. It's the first time we've seen him truly happy since the beginning of the book.

Page 33

Text: Then... what is this?

Illustration: Pip stops and looks down at his body in surprise. A little shimmer of color is starting to appear around him.

Page 34

Text: A little wiggle...

Illustration: Pip's body does a small, gentle wiggle. A few little stars pop out.

Page 35
Text: Then a big wiggle!
Illustration: Pip explodes in a full-body wiggle, even bigger and more colorful than the one at the start of the book.

Page 36
Text: "My wiggle!" said Pip. "It is here!"
Illustration: Pip is wiggling with pure joy. The friendly dog is wagging its tail, looking very pleased.

Page 37
Text: "You see," said the dog. "Your wiggle was not lost."
Illustration: The dog is sitting, looking wise and happy. Pip stopped wiggling for a moment to listen.

Page 38
Text: "Where was it?" said Pip.
Illustration: Pip looks at the dog with a curious and thankful expression.

Page 39
Text: "Your wiggle is in you," said the good dog.
Illustration: The dog gently nudges Pip with its nose. The scene is warm and friendly.

Page 40
Text: "It comes out when you are happy."
Illustration: A beautiful, full-page spread showing Pip and the dog playing. The blue bird, red bug, and green-striped cat are all there, playing with

them. Everyone is happy.

Page 41
Text: Pip has a friend. A lot of friends.
Illustration: Pip is in the middle of a group hug with all his new friends.

Page 42
Text: Pip has his wiggle. His fun, funny wiggle.
Illustration: Pip is wiggling happily as he waves goodbye to his friends at the end of the day.

Page 43
Text: Now Pip is home. The sun is down. The moon is up.
Illustration: Pip is back at his little round home. A big, friendly moon with a sleepy smile is in the sky, along with colorful stars.

Page 44
Text: He is happy. So very happy.
Illustration: Pip is curled up in his little bed, with a big, contented smile on his face. A soft, gentle wiggle is still faintly shimmering around him as he sleeps.

Page 45
Text: Good night, Pip. Good night, wiggle.
Illustration: A final, peaceful image of the outside of Pip's house under the starry, whimsical night sky. A soft, warm light glows from his window.

I used an AI computer program to generate the illustrations. The process was exciting to "think like a child" and create an attention-grabbing book! Stay tuned! Life is a process, and then we die. I want the "dash" on my head stone to reflect a life of doing it, rather than wishing I had done it!

Life as an author is great! My health has improved. My blocked vein in my head has been resolved with further diagnoses that I do not have a blocked vein! My possible brain cancer has been determined to be a benign brain tumor. I will keep an eye on it with frequent check-ups by a neurologist! Life is good at 80 years old! No symptoms!

Dallas W. Thompson

Lakeside, Arizona 85929

dallas93309@gmail.com

www.DallasWThompson.com

www.ingramcontent.com/pod-product-compliance
Lightning Source LLC
Chambersburg PA
CBHW061307110426
42742CB00012BA/2090